Reviving
The Church
In
America

Reviving The Church In America

Do not be afraid nor dismayed by this great multitude, for the battle is not yours, but God's.

Leslie Vann

Xulon Press

Xulon Press
555 Winderley Pl, Suite 225
Maitland, FL 32751
407.339.4217
www.xulonpress.com

Xulon
PRESS

Unless otherwise indicated, Scripture quotations taken from the
King James Version (KJV) – *public domain.*

Paperback ISBN-13: 978-1-66289-427-5
Ebook ISBN-13: 978-1-66289-428-2

The Author

I've been a contractor and homebuilder for most of my adult life. My wife, Katie, and I attend the First Pentecostal Holiness Church in Lumberton, North Carolina, where I serve on the Board. I have no formal education in theology. My understanding of the Christian faith comes only from Bible study, sermons, Sunday school lessons, and prayerful thought.

Over my lifetime I've attended several different denominations—enough to notice that some are steering their congregations toward a change in direction. I'm writing this book because I'm concerned about the influence of false teachings in many churches in America today and want to see the nation return to the faith that comes from a deeply personal love of Christ again.

What This Book Is About

The church was established by Jesus through the work of the Holy Spirit. Jesus has warned us from the beginning that we would face deceptive challenges, and that delusion would be extremely powerful in the last days. We are told in Scripture how to overcome these deceptions and keep our faith in Christ. This book is intended to call believers to an awareness of the spiritual war and the methods being used against us and to remind us of what the Bible says to do when challenged in our faith.

I believe we are on the threshold of a great outpouring of God's Spirit, and He wants the leaders and faithful followers of His church to come together in a more unified and powerful front. I believe we can have a great revival if we follow His lead in faith.

Introduction

A lot of Christians are getting very concerned about the state of the church in America today. It's no wonder when you look around and see how American culture seems to be changing. The Bible tells us that in the last days there will be a great falling away and an apostate church will rise to distract the faithful, and the evidence of this can be seen every day now.

Our moral standards today seem to be based on human secularism and the rules that God has set for worship, family life, and moral conduct are being ignored. The left-leaning media are becoming openly hostile to Christian belief.

Many of the mainstream churches have tried to adapt to a changing society by compromising our beliefs with the world. There are preachers in the pulpit today who don't believe in the virgin birth or divinity of Christ. Many churches are teaching that the Bible is not reliable as the inspired Word from the Holy Spirit.

God never meant for us to be free from challenges to our faith on this earth. When He made Adam and Eve, He allowed the devil to come into the garden to tempt them. Eve, newly created with good human intelligence, had never heard anyone tell a lie before, and it was easy to deceive her into thinking that God was the deceitful one, not the devil. She and Adam quickly learned the hard way which one told the truth, and which one was a liar. And from that day forward, they, and all their descendants, have had to deal with the devil's devices to deceive us away from God.

At various times since the church was founded by our Lord we have gained ground and really shone as a light for Him in this world, and at other times we have stumbled. Many Christians are convinced today that America has now become so enthralled with the ways of the flesh and secular thinking that we can never win many souls back to Christ again. But Christ has provided us with the defenses and the weapon we need to be victorious for Him again.

The key to our victory in faith is His Holy Spirit. Jesus once said that the sons of this age are wiser at their own craft than the sons of light, and with the devil's help, that is true. After His resurrection Jesus told His disciples not to begin the work of evangelizing until they had received the Holy Spirit. We, also, can accomplish nothing without Him.

The devil has his side well fooled and well organized. There is a continual spiritual war being waged on the earth. It is a war to control our minds. It is a war of truth against lies; a war of the One who loves us and wants us to have the things that lead us to our eternal peace versus a liar who would bring us to everlasting ruin.

Jesus tells us that in order to live in peace, harmony, and happiness, we have to observe God's laws to love the Lord our God and our neighbor as ourselves. If you will accept this as what you, as an individual, are responsible for, believe it and trust Him; He will save you and bring you into His kingdom in a new body, free from the fleshly weaknesses that you now live under. He will forgive you of your sins and bring you through this time of temptation if you are sincere.

The devil never makes any promises for the future in his own name. He only tries to keep everyone fooled into thinking that you can't believe in God. He wants to keep you distracted from the very thing that brings you to Christ under the convicting power of the Holy Spirit, the realization of your own personal responsibility. If he can keep you away from that, he can control you.

He has so many fooled in America today that they are beginning an attempt to mandate that the groupthink and the voice that he inspires is the only proper way and any opposing viewpoint needs to be condemned and censured. But the church has not only the right but the commission and responsibility to try to bring the nation back to Christ by every means available to us.

We can't just sit back and not bother anybody because the devil tells us that our opinion is not wanted. He is fervently waging an all-out war for the control of the minds of all men and invading every channel to reach us at our earliest ages.

To win this fight we're going to have to rally the church back to the purpose for which we are called. We're going to have to rally back to the rock that has begotten us as a strongly united front and faithfully follow the direction of the Holy Spirit.

First Peter 5:8 gives us a good picture of how the devil operates in the world; like a roaring lion. When a herd of antelopes are near to a pride of lions after the heat of the day, the female lions stealthily move into position and the male lion begins roaring with the loudest, most threatening, and invincible sound in the world. The scared antelopes run right into the trap.

Propaganda is a powerful tool, and the devil is a powerful influence on many of the main channels of communication in the United States today. Everywhere we look, we already see the sway it is having in the church. We are seeing many succumb to the pressure to accept sexual perversion, men and women living together without the commitment of marriage, Jesus relegated to a purely human position, and every aspect of Christian living that separates us from the world reworked and modified.

The devil has got us right where he wants us. People in America today are about as miserable, from the standpoint of peace of mind, as they've ever been. If he can keep us divided into two groups, each one so obsessed with the idea that the other needs to be destroyed that we don't look for the direction of the Holy Spirit, he has a win-win situation.

What if the herd of antelopes, when they heard the roaring male lion, saw what was going on, and rushed headlong toward his voice and trampled him to death?

The church of Christ needs to wake up and fully realize what is really going on now. A lot of us probably look around and think that it's already too late to change the nation and all we can do is try to be sure we hold on to the faith ourselves. We're acting as if the Holy Spirit gives us no power.

Do you realize that throughout our history the church has never won any to Christ when the devil had not created an environment just as hostile and foreboding as what we face now? When the church first began, the followers of Christ faced more opposition than we do now. When the

Reformation began, they faced more opposition than we do now. In the early days of Colonial America and the United States, many of the people who came here were in search of economic opportunity, not religious freedom. Our vibrant churches came into being because called evangelists believed in Christ, worked with dedication, and entrusted the results of their ministry to the power of the Holy Spirit.

If the church will work in unity, return to the ardent love of Christ, and confront the deceiver under the power and leadership of the Holy Spirit, there can be a great revival in America again!

Chapter 1

Reflections

It is interesting and often surprising to see how much the world can change in one's lifetime. As I write this, I am seventy-nine years old. I was born in 1943, while the Second World War was going on, but of course, I don't remember the war. In some of my oldest memories, I couldn't tell you how old I was, but in the world at the time when I was old enough to have clear recollections, things were far different than they are now.

I remember how, as a small child, I liked to draw pictures of things. I would draw pictures of houses with big windowpanes and steeper roofs than any real ones in the neighborhood and I liked to draw trains. In our dining room, which served more as a den at the time, I could look out the back window across a small field and watch the train stop at the water tower to refill. It was a steam locomotive and that was the train I drew pictures of. I would draw the locomotive with its cab, windows, wheels, smokestack, bell, and cowcatcher. Next came the coal car, box cars, and then the red caboose. The railroads and steam locomotives were still a main means of transportation at that time. My grandfather had a woodwork shop across the street from the depot and one time when I was at his shop he got the engineer, Mr. Odom, to let me ride in the cab to the Y to turn the train around.

The two main highways that crossed at the downtown business district were paved and there were concrete sidewalks on both sides of Broad Street, Hwy 87, for about nine blocks. The business district had a sidewalk on both sides of Hwy 701 and one side of Ben Street for one block. The rest of the streets were not paved.

We lived on King Street, which ran parallel to Broad. There was a path about 18 inches wide that extended down King Street a few feet off the street through everyone's front yard, right by their front porch, to walk downtown or to school and back.

In my earliest memories a lot of people owned an automobile, but then there was only a tiny fraction of the number of cars on the roads than there are now. There was a man who made a living, hauling things that were shipped by rail to the train station to persons and businesses around the area and there was a bus station and a taxicab. There were transfer trucks, but they were not as big as the ones you see now and nowhere near as many. You would occasionally see a horse and wagon, but they were fast becoming obsolete. There were school buses as far back as I can remember. The main state and federal highways were paved but most roads in rural areas were not.

At the time I was born, the economy in southeastern North Carolina was mainly based on agriculture. There were two lumber mills and one plant that was involved with processing peanuts in Elizabethtown.

Some farmers owned tractors but most still had mules and horses to plow, plant, and harvest crops. The main crops raised commercially were tobacco, cotton, and peanuts. Most rural areas didn't have electricity. Hand pumps and wells were a common site and if a farmer had electric lights, he had to have a generator. I can remember my uncle Edwin referring to his generator in a little enclosure on the side of the house as his "light plant."

Communication was also far different. I can remember our next-door neighbor having a car before we did, but they came to our house to use the telephone. Our telephone was the old type that had the round dial, and the receiver hung on a hook. Our telephone listing consisted of three numbers. If you called someone out of town, you had to dial the operator and agree to pay the charges for long distance.

People used to write letters to friends and relatives who lived in other parts of the country. I don't know exactly when ballpoint pens became available, but I can remember my mother writing letters when you had to buy ink in little jars to use in your pens. She would write to her brother and his wife in Tacoma Park, Maryland, to her uncle Sydney, the brother of her deceased mother, in San Diego, and to others who lived closer by that we didn't see often. It seems like I can remember postage stamps being one or two cents.

No one had a television back then. Radio was the main means of communication and entertainment. There were newscasts and of course advertising but what I remember best was comedy and drama programs. I remember listening to *Jack Benny, Our Miss Brooks, Amos and Andy, Gildersleeve,*

Fibber McGee and Molly, The Green Hornet, and *Gunsmoke.* I also remember listening to The Grand Ole Opry, and country music on WCKY in Cincinnati.

A lot of people didn't lock their doors at night back then, and no one had an alarm system. I don't remember anyone keeping their dog penned up or on a leash except one man about a block away who had some special dogs he used for bear hunting.

On Halloween some of us would get together and go trick or treating by ourselves and we would go to every house in town. When I was just old enough to join the Boy Scouts, a friend of mine, who was about a year older, and I decided to hike to Clarkton and back, about ten miles away, to earn a merit badge. Today, I'm sure it would raise some eyebrows to hear that parents allowed two boys that young to hike down a federal highway like that. I remember that when we got to Clarkton a nice lady spotted us from her porch and invited us to come and sit down and have a coke. She said that she saw us and thought that we must be scouts on a hike. I was probably in my mid 30s when I was reminiscing with my friend and we recalled that time and, for the first time, it dawned on us that she was supposed to be watching for us!

A lot of boys, by the time we were twelve years old or so, had a .22 rifle or a .410 shotgun and were allowed to go hunting in the river lowlands. To this day, I couldn't tell you whose land we were on. It never occurred to any of us at the time that it belonged to anybody. In our neighborhood, we boys usually took the shortest route to go anywhere and that was often down the Hemingway's drive to a path that led through the Jessup's back yard, right by their back door.

If we were going to the river lowlands to play that was often through Dr. Glenn's yard to a path in the woods.

The old-time country general store still existed at that time. Many small communities where there was a cross-roads had one where they sold gasoline, soft drinks and snacks, a few grocery and clothing articles, and such things as fertilizer and hog feed.

Saturday was the big day for merchants in town because that was when the farmers all came to town to buy goods, get haircuts, and so forth. The downtown parking spaces were filled with farmers' vehicles and the sidewalks with farmers and their families socializing. The theater was a big source of entertainment for children on Saturday afternoon. There was usually a double feature of westerns with our favorite cowboys. My favorite was Roy Rogers. Admission was only a dime. A bag of popcorn was a dime, and a fountain coke was a nickel. We got our money's worth. There was always a cartoon or two and sometimes a serial to keep us coming back for the next episode. The theaters were always packed with children for the matinees.

My father was a carpenter. At the time of my earliest memories, most sawing was done with handsaws. Miter cuts were done with a handsaw in a homemade wooden miter box. Holes were drilled with a hand turned brace and bit. Screws were put in with a handheld screwdriver and nails were hammered. Walls and roofs were sheathed with 1" x 6" boards instead of plywood sheets.

My mother's father ran a woodwork shop where he built cabinets, window and door screens, and the like. He had electric table saws, planes, and band saws. He also did a considerable business sharpening handsaws for carpenters.

To sharpen a handsaw so that it doesn't tend to pull to one side or the other requires a great deal of skill and my grandfather was very good at it. In the carpentry trade, they had to work harder and develop skills that are no longer commonplace and that is true of a lot of other professions as well.

I also remember a couple of relics from a bygone era in my early years. Just behind and to the left of my grandfather's shop was an old blacksmith shop that still had anvils, bellows, and all the other tools that blacksmiths used. The man who used to run it was, I believe, a cousin of my grandfather. The man who lived just across the street from us ran an Esso gasoline station downtown and just behind his station was an old livery stable.

Throughout the rest of my life, we have seen amazing changes and progress. Air travel, which was launched here in North Carolina when my father was about three years old, became commonplace, with jet airplanes reducing travel time to a small fraction of what it used to be.

We've sent men to the moon and back. Our homes are now well insulated and air conditioned. Growing up in the 1950s, I didn't know anyone who lived in an air-conditioned home. Public buildings now have automatic doors. We're all familiar with automatic faucets, hand driers, automatic lights, TV remotes, smart appliances, microwaves, the internet, smart phones, credit cards, checkout scanners, ATMs, and little robot floor cleaners. We didn't have any of these things when I was small.

Satellites now circle the earth to observe weather conditions and most any visible thing that happens on earth. When you go somewhere in your car you can listen to a voice that knows exactly where you are and tells you when and where to make turns. Instead of a little tractor pulling a six foot or so wide disc, a farmer now sits in the air-conditioned cab of a huge tractor pulling equipment of enormous spread, guided by satellite precisely regulating his pattern of preparation, planting, and delivering the right number of fertilizers and other treatments for specific areas.

Automobiles are now easier and more comfortable to drive and are more fuel efficient. When I learned to drive there were still a lot of cars on the road in which you had to roll the window down to give a hand-signal to turn. Those old cars used twice as much fuel as modern cars do now.

I was born in Lumberton because there was no hospital in Bladen County at that time. There were two doctors in Elizabethtown that I remember when I was a little boy. Our family doctor had an office in a small brick building a half block from our house. By the time I was a teenager we'd had a hospital built in Elizabethtown. Today you can ride through the wealthiest section of Lumberton and see a few homes that look larger to me than the hospital I was born in, which has long since been replaced with a modern hospital that is many times larger.

Instead of a few doctors who could reset broken bones, remove tonsils, and prescribe medicines for several illnesses we now have an army of highly trained specialists doing everything from brain and heart surgery to joint replacements and a multitude of things that we had never heard of seventy years ago. There are medicines to treat just about every condition you've ever heard of and many new ones coming out to treat conditions that you haven't heard of yet.

I remember when the local doctors would make house calls to sick people, bringing their little black bags with stethoscopes, thermometers, tongue depressors, etc. Now you go to them if there's anything wrong with you and they send you somewhere for an MRI, CAT scan, or other testing. They can shatter kidney stones, put a stint in a clogged artery, install a pacemaker to regulate your heartbeat, replace bones with artificial parts, do surgery with very small incisions, perform surgery with robots, and many other things that we couldn't imagine seventy years ago. The main health problem we have today is that many of us don't get enough exercise to keep us healthy.

The environment is now much healthier in many ways. Every municipality used to have a city dump that was rat infested and now waste is disposed of in a less polluting manner. A lot of sewerage used to be dumped directly into the rivers and now the entire ecosystem is protected. More and more electricity is produced with low carbon emission methods and new cars and trucks are held to a higher standard of emissions. Electric and hybrid cars are already being produced in appreciable numbers.

I can remember when the "Welfare" department of the county government system was one small room in the courthouse, financed by a very small fraction of overall federal spending. Today, The Department of Social Services consists of several buildings and numerous employees with a substantial segment of the population receiving regular checks, housing, food stamps, and other support.

Compared to the living standard of three quarters of a century ago, most of us today are actually rich. Yet, it seems that the average person is less content with their quality of life now than they were then. We have an enormous host of trained psychologists, counselors, and psychiatrists staffing public and private facilities everywhere, and yet, far more people are living with depression, despair, and a sense of discontent. Death from drug overuse, which used to be rare, is now reaching epidemic proportions.

Why is this? It's certainly not because we have more and better things. I doubt that any of us would want to give up our more comfortable homes, better transportation, or higher living standards that we have because we thought it would bring back the "good old days."

Chapter 2

Cherished Memories

M y first playmate and I have many cherished memories of the past. I've only seen him a few times in the last thirty or so years, but on the rare occasions when our paths cross, we have spent many hours fondly reminiscing about the past, mainly the oldest memories we have when we were little boys.

The level of affluence we had at the time has nothing to do with making cherished memories. At the time, it never occurred to us whether we were rich or not. Through our shared memories we cherish what we were, not what we had, and in the present, we can only find fulfillment in what we are, not what we have.

The making of cherished memories, though we are not fully cognizant of it at the time, also involves others. As small children, we were aware that we lived in a world run by adults, and we were dependent on them to lead us. Because we believed in them and trusted that the ways they led us in were right, our world was stable. Even at that early age, we were to some degree aware that our parents were not perfect or wholly righteous, but we could sense their sincerity toward us, and we knew that their motivation was right. It was a far more personal world, and children could sense that their right development was important to most adults.

There is something about us at every age that just knows when we are being led and can sense whether we are following the right or wrong, and we can sense that there is a spirit within us that knows this. We can sense that we are part of and belong to the one who wants to lead us in the right path. When we don't, we inevitably experience a feeling of unease and anxiety. No matter how much glitz and glamour are waved in front of us, we can still sense that the end is not secure.

This is true whether we are adults or small children and dependent on the guidance of adults. That is why the Bible puts so much emphasis on family and organized worship. God knows that we must understand and practice the roles that he has given us and that they must be made a part of our society and culture to encourage us to follow the path of blessing and inner peace, rather than the path that leads to unease and anxiety.

Because there is something about us of a rebellious nature that resents any constraints on our carnal appetites, we need to live in a society that keeps us constantly reminded of our responsibility to follow the right spirit and that reminds us of the result of failing to do so. The Bible makes it plain that we have the duty, not to just be Christians ourselves, but to strive to bring the message to society around us. We are supposed to create and maintain a Christian culture, to practice it ourselves, and to indoctrinate our children. (Matt. 28:16-20) (Prov. 22:6)

Frankly, I would not want to be a small child or a parent in charge of raising children in this society we have in America today. When my childhood friend and I were small we were seeing an entirely different world, and it was far better than what children are seeing now. By the time we were more than just toddlers and had inquiring minds we understood that not all the adults in the world were perfect, and certainly not all were Christians, but we saw our society as one where God was acknowledged and respected. Sunday was a day of rest from this world and attending church. It certainly never occurred to us that our parents might get a divorce, and our homes would be broken up. We saw them as people who believed in God and accepted responsibility for our upbringing. Nothing about the media and general culture that we were exposed to would lead us to believe that we, as a society, rejected the good sense and rightness of Christian principles. We truly believed that we should be thankful that we lived in a free nation and that we should all cherish and be glad that we had the right to worship as we believed was right.

This is not the world that many children in this nation are seeing today. Every day the full force of a greatly expanded news and entertainment media and academia is blaring out loudly that organized worship is a divisive idea of the unenlightened past, and that man's future lies in a unified secular, socialist world.

The thing that caused children to feel secure in our society in the past was the belief that the adults who ran things were morally strong, and would see to it that right would prevail, making sure that the same strength would be instilled in us. Now, everything has been shifted around.

Family life and the roles of men and women in its makeup is all out of whack. Instead of the voice of authority from parents and other involved adults stressing individual responsibility to the children to develop strength of character, children today are more exposed to the media steering them to rely on society with their stress on "political correctness" for guidance. The rules of responsibility that God gave us has been cast aside.

Sunday is now a big day at the mall. A smaller percentage of the people now attend church and some of the mainstream churches no longer accept the belief in divine inspiration of the Scriptures or the divinity of Christ. Marriage is no longer deemed sacred. Premarital sex and living together unwed is now accepted and portrayed by the media as the norm. Abortion to get rid of unwanted children is labeled a right. Homosexuality and lesbianism are spun by the media as perfectly normal and acceptable lifestyles and are highlighted at every opportunity.

What do you think goes on in the formulative minds of America's little children now? Little children are dependent on adults, but they still sense it when they are put on an insecure path, even if the adults leading them have become hardened to ignore the warning signs. Their surroundings greatly affect them when their perception of moral character begins to form. They need guidance to develop faith in following the right path and feel helpless without it. They are not supposed to be able to do this on their own.

We have become a society that leaves many of them robbed of the feeling of security they need for healthy growth because so many of us have run away from God. The only way to avoid certain destruction is to return to

Him. If we do that, the next generation will not grow up in an atmosphere that leaves them bewildered and lost, but can have spiritual health, faith, and many cherished memories.

Chapter 3

The forgotten God

M any in America have forgotten God. We need revival, but we have let so many in America forget God that there needs to first be a revival of the knowledge of God, before there can be a revival of worship. Any time one generation loses devotion to God, the next one doesn't know Him.

Before we can be revived, we need to know who God is and how He relates to us. We need to know who Jesus is, who the Holy Spirit is, who the devil is, and who we are. Many, even in some of the main churches in America today, don't know. And when we speak of revival, we need to understand that revival means bringing to life the spirit that we have within us. The Bible says, "God is a spirit and those who worship Him must worship Him in spirit and truth" (John 4:24. The most chaotic thing that happens when people have abandoned God is that because they still subconsciously believe that there must be one, they begin to invent in their own minds a god as they think they want Him to be. He has already told us what He is like and how to reach Him, but they have lost track of that. They no longer understand that He can be acknowledged and invited into our lives, and the god they invent is more distant, allowing a little space to suit the carnal nature of man.

Unaware that they even have a spiritual nature themselves, the god they invent has no spiritual nature either, and simply leaves it to them to pick and choose their own lifestyle and concepts of right and wrong, a god at arm's length. They don't establish boundaries that don't please their carnal nature. It never occurs to them that God might have something to say about it.

They wind up with a god who is not kin to us. They have invented a god with whom they have no personal relationship, and they don't want one until they need him. When they do feel a need for their new god, if he doesn't do their bidding, they are disappointed in him. Then they don't know whether to believe he doesn't exist, or he simply doesn't care.

They blame Him for not caring and act as if their childish accusations should move Him to prove Himself by doing what they want. They've lost contact. God has provided the way to reach Him, but they are unaware because the god in their minds has been reinvented and they are ignorant of God's provision, thinking that they must come to Him in their own way when they need Him.

They have no concept of the true spiritual nature of God because they have ignored all communication that He has provided through the Holy Spirit, and they are unaware of what the Bible says about Him.

When a person reaches that state, the possibility that He can be found in inspired Word or Scripture is shut out. When the inevitable time comes that he needs God for something, he wants to unilaterally offer God a chance to prove Himself, either revealing His existence by overwhelming him with a bullying show of force, or by supernaturally granting his request to suit his carnal nature. But God is the molder and maker of our spiritual nature and will never be found that way.

For the moment let's set aside the Bible and the literature of any other religion and ask ourselves if there is any purely secular, scientific reason to believe in the existence of God. As you ponder that, ask yourself this: What are you doing now? You're thinking.

What exactly is thought? We are all part of a physical universe. Our bodies are physical and everything we can see is physical. We can't see through a wall or walk through a tree. Our thoughts seem to originate in our brains but isn't there something about thought that seems different from the rest of the physical universe?

We are all aware that our thoughts are somehow tied to our physical bodies. If we are deprived of air long enough, we will become unconscious. We know that our ability to think can be impaired by dementia or brain damage.

We all know some people who have exceptionally good memory, powers of reasoning, or mathematical abilities. We all interact with others through thought. All the emotions we experience come through thought.

Even though we know that all of these need a functioning brain and nervous system, there is still something about thought that is different from anything else in the physical realm. Could it be that our brains are designed to simulate something else?

The universe consists of two basic types of things: conscious things and unconscious things. Unconscious things include objects, such as the stars, planets, asteroids, etc., and there is a force that holds these objects in place and on course. Whatever that is can't be seen but we know it must be there.

The earth spins around every day, stays about 93 million miles from the sun, circling around it every year, tilting back and forth in the same pattern to bring the seasons during the annual circuit. The moon circles the earth in the same pattern and all the planets follow their same orbit. We are all flying around at an incredible rate of speed and yet, to our perception we're standing still. Every day we are moving somewhere around two million miles a day in orbit. If you stood at a pole all day you would simply turn around and at the equator you would move another 25,000 or so miles.

We don't really know what gravity is, but it has to exist everywhere. A lot of scientific research has been done but much still remains a mystery. If we really understood all the properties of gravity and knew exactly its source and how it works, we could probably travel enormous distances and lift incredibly heavy objects without using fuel.

Is outer space nothing, through which some type of force travels that activates gravity as an inward pull while moving the heavenly objects in a pattern or does it have some type of physical property itself to coordinate with all the innumerable objects moving in the universe?

If outer space is not nothing, what exactly is nothing? In the entire physical universe, there is really no such thing as nothing. Nothing is simply everything that doesn't exist.

Space exists. We measure distance through it. If you google outer space, it is described as containing a low density of particles, predominately plasma of hydrogen and helium, as well as electronic radiation, magnetic fields, neutrinos, dust, and cosmic rays. You don't see any structure, but it is there. Nothing, in the real sense, wouldn't be there.

What exactly is consciousness? All the lower animals think. Much of what they do is controlled by instinct. My dictionary defines that term as an innate, automatic impulse, in humans and animals, to satisfy basic biological needs, leading to behavior that is purposeful and directive; an involuntary tendency or drive to act in a specific way under given conditions.

All the lower animals have this, but it is a physical type of consciousness. Something just put into their minds' genes causes them to behave or react to stimulus in a certain way. They don't know why they do it, they just do. They have memory and can be conditioned in youth by imitation, which comes naturally by a built-in sense of belonging to a parent. They are also conditioned by fondness and affection or fear of other animals.

I once had a dog that seemed to be dearly beloved by everyone in the neighborhood. He was a very good-looking dog and one of the neighbors said that he was the most "sociable" dog she'd ever seen. When my wife got him from the pound they described the mother as a miniature collie, but he grew to be larger than anything you would call miniature. I always thought that he probably inherited the genes of a sheep herding dog because I would see him, while running, jump high and turn his head, as if looking over a herd of sheep.

He broke his front leg and spent the rest of his life with a limp leg. I wish I could have gotten him to the vet sooner, but it probably wouldn't have helped. When it happened, it was the evening of the second day before I found him. The first day, I called and searched and looked for him but couldn't find him. When I finally found him, he was hidden under the house.

I think he did that because of instinct. Winston considered himself to be part of the family and reason would have told him to come to me for help as soon as he heard or saw me. But instead, he behaved like an injured wolf, finding a quiet, safe place to hide while his injuries could heal.

Why does a heron stand still in the edge of a pond waiting for a minnow to come by while ducks and geese swim around? Why does each generation of birds know to build a nest and how to do it? How do beavers know how to build dams and why do they do it? How do migrating birds know which way is south and why do geese fly in formation? Animals that do things essential to their survival don't do it because of wise planning and practicing. They do what they do and live where they live because of a type of consciousness, and that is a type of physical consciousness that is just part of their genetic makeup. It is passed on from generation to generation, not learned. The only thing that seems to be learned is how to kill prey among carnivorous animals.

We belong to a higher order of consciousness. Only we think in language. We reason and analyze, we store more in memory, we experience deeper emotions, and we have a natural desire to master the world around us, to visualize the future, and to be able to control our fate. We are not satisfied with just living out our lives; we want to understand the universe around us; to know how things work and why.

No one can ponder the things that come naturally to our minds without asking the most fundamental question; how did it all start? It just seems to be an elemental fact to us that everything must have a beginning.

When we think about the universe with its countless burning stars, their satellites, light, energy forces, gravity, and unseen controls that cause everything to follow a pattern, it doesn't make sense to say that it just always existed. And if the universe "evolved" into what it is now over a period of countless eons, where did whatever it is made of come from?

The most prevalent theory among the world's most prominent scientists who study cosmology to explain the beginning of the universe is the "Big Bang" theory. This is the only theory that offers a reasonable hypothesis that is consistent with everything known about the behavior of all the known forces in the universe. According to this, the universe began as something about the size of a peach which exploded into rapid expansion because of intense heat. Everything you see in the universe with all its stars burning in indescribable heat for eons began as this, and it is still expanding.

Now let's think a little outside the box for a moment. Your focus when you muse over the big bang theory tends to be on that tiny peach sized thing and it exploding and expanding. But now think about this; expanding into what? If you could ride the outer waves of the universe as it expands at a growing rate, what would you see out there? What is nothing and what are its boundaries? How did something the size of a peach which became hot enough to explode and expand forever, forming stars of millions of degrees of heat get that hot in nothing? In all of nothing, which goes on forever boundless, where did this peach sized genetic pattern for the universe come from?

So, did conscious perception and thought begin before or after something was formed in nothing? If there were no consciousness would anything really exist? If you've never thought about it before, it may seem to be amusing in a weird sort of way, but without consciousness, time, space, distance, or boundaries of any kind would not exist.

We all have human consciousness, but ours is really just a simulated form of consciousness. The kind of consciousness that we have could not create the universe from nothing.

So, who is God? I think that almost anyone, if he thinks about it long enough, will conclude that it is unlikely that the unconscious universe would have just always existed before conscious thought existed to perceive it. It was created.

To most of us it is hard to imagine what the nature of the creator of the universe would have to be. We tend to subconsciously think that all the things that limit us would also limit Him. But, if this universe was created, it must have been created by a conscious, intelligent being of another dimension. His consciousness could not have any limitations to create something that stays together in an orderly fashion and seems to continue forever. With Him time, space, and distance do not exist. He is always everywhere. This is unimaginable to us, but it must be true. Everything created comes from the original consciousness, the mind of God.

When you consider that if God exists, he must have the power to create the whole universe and know the individual thoughts of billions of people in real time, you have to realize that it is doubtful that we would ever prove or disprove Him with our scientific research. But if He did make us and gave us the gift of conscious thought, and that gift bears a resemblance to His conscious thought, then the best hope we have of finding Him is if He has done or said anything to reveal Himself to us.

He has and it is revealed to us in the Bible. But I want you, as we begin looking at His revelation, to seriously ask yourself this; why has He allowed so much opposition and deception in the world to keep that revelation from us? Understanding that is paramount to your full understanding, not just of who He is, but who we are and the purpose for which He has made us—to grow into something better.

He has the power to force every one of us to submit to His will, or even control our thoughts and make us be anything He wants us to be, but that is not what He does. Instead, He has revealed Himself in Christ and allowed the evil forces of this world to challenge His word and attempt to deceive and corrupt us because He wants us to grow into His nature.

You can never understand God if you don't realize that He is entirely different from the physical creatures that we are. He has a different nature. This is a nature that cannot be seen with the physical eye.

He created you to begin life as a physical creature, but to become a spiritual being in His likeness, and the work He performs to change you is not done like work done in a laboratory but like a father who is thinking and helping shape the man you will become. The change from your carnal body is already built in and your carnal body will die and disappear. Everything He says to you is to the spirit within you; to develop the inner you to become like Him.

If He invented seeds so that plants live and die and reproduce, and male and female animals to reproduce and die, He can also make us to live on with another nature. And if there is only one right way to do that, that will help us become what's best for us. He would know that, and He wouldn't offer you anything less. But you must understand that your path of eternal blessing is an offer that you must accept. You have to acknowledge Him and let Him in to finish His work.

There is every reason in the world for you to believe that there is a God. He is real and He has spoken to us and provided us with the way to find Him personally. He has provided the way that is best for you to come to Him, and you must believe Him and come that way. You will never find Him your own way. Open up to Him.

Chapter 4

What Is the Bible About?

The Bible wastes no time in getting to the point of what it is about. The first thing it tells us is that God created the heavens and the earth. Somewhere in our minds, consciously or subconsciously, we all know that nothing physical just always existed. It had to start somewhere, and God said it all started when He made it.

As you begin to ponder the Bible version of creation, I want you to bear this in mind. I am a fundamentalist, and the things I express here are from a fundamentalist viewpoint. There has been a great, well-orchestrated effort underway for many decades to portray Christian fundamentalism, through every available channel, as irrational simplemindedness and ignorance of science.

But fundamentalism really comes from deep thought, reasoning, and examination of the Bible in consideration of what we know or think we know about science. *Fundamental* means foundational. The foundation of our faith is spiritual. It is the belief that God exists and that He made us for a spiritual purpose. Fundamentalist thought is based on the message that a spiritual God has given us, not physical proof of any kind.

The entire theme of the Bible is found right in the first three chapters. When you read them, try not to read them like a fairy tale, but as a revelation from an omnipotent God who is not limited by space, distance, or time. Moses, who recorded it and spoke with God face-to-face, said that to the Lord, a thousand years is as but a day or a watch in the night. Time means nothing to Him. He knows what happened a million years ago and He will be no older than He is now in another million.

Don't focus on the term *day* to determine whether you think the Bible creation story is credible. The term *day* is often used metaphorically in the Bible for an era. We really have no idea from Genesis' description how long these things took. Genesis 2:4 gives a recap saying, "These are the generations of the heavens and the earth when they were created, in the day that the Lord made the earth and the heavens." So here the whole thing that is first described in seven stages or days is now described as a day.

Focus instead on the order of the generation of the earth as a planet and remember that this was written around 3500 years ago. What do you think the science of that day taught about creation and cosmology? Clearly, it was told by someone who saw the earth as a planet being formed; one among countless other heavenly objects held in space to a fixed place and pattern by a force that He created. After God made the heavens, which includes the stars and our sun, the Bible describes the changes that occurred as the earth became what it is today.

At first, it was in a more nebulous form instead of the solid sphere that it is now. Thick vapors surrounded whatever became the earth and it was dark on the "face of the deep." The spirit of the Lord was moving on this. When He said, "Let there be light," He was not creating light. The light was created first with the heavens, but then it began to become visible on the "face of the deep."

The second day, the sky with its atmosphere was formed with water below and water or vapor above. The dry land and seas emerged on the third day and plant life began. Next, the pattern of light from the sun and moon was established, then marine life, land animals, and finally man were created.

The history of the formation of the earth actually goes back immeasurably farther than the scope of modern science in the evolution of the earth. No serious scientist can honestly refute this account with what real knowledge we have of cosmology. Not everyone who is considered a credible scientific cosmology expert accepts the big bang theory. There is really no way to prove or disprove it. What we accept with more certainty comes after the beginnings of the universe and is derived from a study of changes that occurred after the earth was completely formed and it assumes that such things as the rate of change, as dated by carbon testing, has not changed.

The difference between the Bible account and what is taught by science (knowledge), in the modern educational system, is that the Bible specifically says that God created man instead of us having evolved from a lower life form.

Genesis 1:11 says, "And God said, Let the earth bring forth vegetation, the herb yielding seed, and the fruit tree yielding fruit, whose seed was in itself, upon the earth; and it was so" Verses 24 and 25 say, "and God said, Let the earth bring forth the living creature after its kind, cattle and creeping things and beast of the earth after its kind, and God saw that it was good."

Next, in verse 26, notice the difference in the way God identifies Himself, "And God said, let us make man in Our image, after Our likeness."

This account was given to Moses by God. Moses once described God as having more than one part, the Shekinah, or glory, which he could not even look upon, himself, and live, and again God could appear to him as one with whom he spoke mouth to mouth, and face-to-face, as a man speaks with his friend.

This is the One of whom John said, "In the beginning was the Word, and the Word was with God, and the Word was God" (John 1:1). This is the One created of God before the beginning, the pattern for us, through whom God intends to work for us to bring us to completion, and that is why He would say, "Let Us make man in Our image" (Gen. 1:26).

Genesis 2:7 says, "And the Lord formed man out of the dust of the ground and breathed into his nostrils the breath of life; and man became a living soul."

The evolution of the earth into the planet it is now may have taken millions of years, for all I know, but I believe that the events described after the creation of man moved right along at a rapid clip. These events, described in the first three chapters of Genesis, preface the entire text of the Bible.

God created man, specifically the first one, Adam, from the dust of the earth. He had a carnal body, but also God created him after His own likeness. So, he had something about him of a spiritual nature, or consciousness. He put Adam into the garden of Eden to tend it and told him that he could eat the fruit of all but one of the trees, the tree of the knowledge of good and evil.

Here, again, we come to the term *day* being used metaphorically. God warned Adam that in the "day" thou eatest thereof thou shalt surely die.

He meant that after Adam had transgressed, all men, having inherited the nature of the first man, would know both good and evil, live under the power of sin, and would experience death. God already knew what would happen in Eden and had planned for it.

When God made the first woman, he did it in a different manner from any other of His creations. He put Adam into a deep sleep, removed a rib, and made the woman from the rib. He did this because He intended to make the woman with some unique features, unlike all the other female creatures. Most other females were also made smaller with less physical force and strength than the males and with maternal instincts. They were made mainly to reproduce their own kind.

The woman was uniquely crafted to be the perfect mate for the man. She was made to be far more attractive to the man physically than female animals to the males, and also to be the perfect spiritual companion. God intended for men and women to live together in a special bond that was fundamentally different from the other creatures. Eve was created for Adam's spiritual health and nourishment, as well as his carnal need for companionship.

As the creation story develops, it seems obvious to me that God knew what would happen in Eden.

When God made Eve in the second chapter and brought her to Adam, he was very happy and said, "This is now bone of my bones and flesh of my flesh. She shall be called woman because she was taken out of man." The next two verses say, "Therefore shall a man leave his father and his mother and shall cleave unto his wife; and they shall be one flesh. And they were both naked, the man and his wife, and were not ashamed." (Gen.3: 24-25)

Now, here God made it plain that He intended them to have a physical sexual relationship and is instituting marriage as the way to do that. But I don't believe for a moment that God ever thought it might be that mankind would fill the earth naked and unashamed, blissfully ignorant of the differences and consequences of good and evil. He allowed the devil to bring his corrupting deception into Eden right away.

God made them with a carnal nature but also a spiritual nature. When they were first created there was nothing causing conflict between the two natures. They were perfectly innocent. But the devil knew that they had never been lied to before and would fall for his lie because it is easy to stir up pride in the carnal nature.

As soon as they fell for the deception, the inner conflict between the two natures began. The carnal nature is vain and pursues pride, always putting self first and seeking to justify any act or feeling toward others that would make us feel wronged if it were directed toward us. Everyone from Adam to now has been unable to overcome sin because of this. The carnal man is always ready to blame whoever "started" it but unable to resist the same sin himself.

The biblical account in Genesis is a perfect illustration of how sin controls us while we have our carnal natures.

From then to now all men have lived in a world overwhelmed with insanity and sin and the root of all that sin is just as simple as the first one in Genesis.

The first thing Adam and Eve experienced after the encounter with the devil was a feeling of shame at their own nakedness. This simple event tells us what we need to know to understand sin: the dread of being seen "naked." God, who is spirit, is totally open, but as long as we have the carnal nature, we know that there is something about us that we don't want seen in the perfect light.

When we talk to God in prayer, we know that we can do it in silence. Even our thoughts are not hidden from Him. We want to have it this way when we need Him, but the carnal man wants the rest of his thoughts to be his own because he knows his own nature. We can never be fully open with each other or with ourselves.

We believe others to be like ourselves and rightly so. Thus, sin becomes automatically reactionary to our own nature. We don't have to go around actively breaking God's commandments for sin to proliferate. Sin is not just the commitment of moral wrongs. Sin is our condition. We all have it, and because of that the whole world has been overrun with sin from the day that Adam and Eve were deceived.

The only way to live sinless is to live in perfect light, honestly valuing others as highly as ourselves. This is what we already demand of others when we judge them, and this is the standard we believe God to have. Because we perceive Him this way and also see Him as our Maker who holds absolute power over our fate, our carnal nature has a sense of dread of "nakedness" before Him. It is in our subconscious to know ourselves. We inwardly know there is no spiritual blindness. The spirit sees everything, but the carnal nature knows our temptations and wants to hide some of the truth. When others do or say something that hurts us, are we not just as hurt by what they thought about us as what they did?

Fortunately for us, God knew what He was doing when He made us to have to live first in the carnal nature of Adam. The provision for our salvation and the transformation was already there before creation. God would not have made us without it.

In the third chapter of Genesis, after Adam and Eve disobeyed God and ate the forbidden fruit, they became conscious of their nakedness and hid themselves among the trees when God called. When God asked if they had eaten the forbidden fruit, Adam blamed Eve and Eve blamed the serpent.

After God told them what their punishment would be He cursed the serpent saying, "And I will put enmity between thee and the woman and between thy seed and her seed. He (the seed of the woman) will bruise thy head and thou shalt bruise his heel." (Gensis 3:15)

The seed of the woman is the spirit of God, revealed in Jesus. It was God's purpose from the beginning that He would save us from sin and bring us to the fullness of the nature of the children of God by trusting in Him. And that is what the whole Bible is about.

Chapter 5

Who Is Jesus?

Human history begins with the words, "Let Us make man in Our image, after Our likeness" (Gen. 1:26). To understand who Jesus is, you must first perceive who God is, for They are the same. God is omnipotent and omnipresent, far beyond our powers of full comprehension. Don't limit Him to what you can easily comprehend and don't limit your perception of Jesus to being only a man.

Jesus lived a life as a man, but only because He limited His own powers for facing temptation to no more that you and I have. He fully experienced human life, but He was also God. When Thomas saw Him resurrected and touched His wounds he exclaimed, "My Lord and my God." (John 20:28)Thomas never really understood that while he was with Him and the other disciples before then.

John, the beloved disciple, begins his account with these words, "In the beginning was the Word, and the Word was God. The same was in the beginning with God. All things were made by Him; and without Him was nothing made that was made. In Him was life; and the life was the light of men" (John 1:1). He came to complete an original purpose for which we were created, and He is the Creator as well as the Finisher.

In Luke 24:25–26 the resurrected Lord said, "O foolish ones, and slow of heart to believe all that the prophets have spoken! Ought not Christ to have suffered those things, and to enter into His glory?"

And beginning with Moses and throughout all the prophets, He expounded unto them, in all the Scriptures, the things concerning Himself.

When He walked among us, He was as fully human as we are. So much so that none of the disciples who were with Him daily fully understood who He was until He was resurrected.

The Bible ascribes many of the characteristics of God to Jesus. Like God the Father, He was not limited by time. John says this,

> Your father Abraham, rejoiced to see my day; and he saw it and was glad.
> Then said the Jews to him, Thou are not yet fifty years old, and hast thou seen Abraham?
> Jesus said unto them, Verily, verily, I say unto you, Before Abraham was, I am.
> (John 8:55–58)

He holds the power of life and death. He didn't have to come as soon as man fell to sin to save sinners. The dead all exist to Him as well as the living. He raised Lazarus from the dead back to the same carnal body, but He has the power to raise us all to new spiritual bodies.

He has authority to forgive sins. Matthew 9:2–6 says,

> And behold, they brought to Him a man sick with the palsy, lying on a bed: and Jesus, seeing their faith, said son, be of good cheer; thy sins be forgiven thee. And certain of the scribes said within themselves, this man blasphemeth. And Jesus, knowing their thoughts, said, why think ye evil in your hearts? For which is easier, to say, thy sins be forgiven thee; or to say, arise and walk? But that ye may know that the Son of Man hath power to forgive sins (then sayeth He to the sick of palsy), arise, take up thy bed, and go unto thy house. And he arose and went unto his house.

He spoke with authority. Matthew 7:29 says, "For he taught them as one having authority, and not as one of the scribes." He always spoke with absolute certainty. He said that He came to fulfill the law, not to change it; He was the author of the law and the prophets. Before him the prophets spoke of one to come and after Him, the prophecy ceased.

His purpose in living as a man on earth is to free all who will trust Him from sin, and give eternal, abundant life. He has full authority from God the Father, of whom He is part Himself, over man and the earth. He is God's appointed king.

Even though God owes us nothing, He justifies His kingly authority by requiring a sacrifice that, by our own standards, meets the highest requirement of worthiness to both us and God, even under all the pressure from the devil, which He allowed while under all human limitations.

Don't misread the term *sacrifice*. To us, a sacrifice is thought of as something that man, in his carnal nature, releases or gives up. It is always something that carnal nature values or prizes, and, in the imagination of his evil heart, shows sincere intention. Man, still sins, even while making a sacrifice, and God knows that sacrifice, in the way we perceive it, will never remove sin. The sacrifice that Jesus made was to not give in to the carnal nature of man toward those sinning against Him. He put God's laws first at the cost of suffering and death. The very most that He has allowed Satan to tempt us with, He experienced Himself, laying our sins on Himself.

From the very beginning, the devil has held us all in bondage and the world was overrun with sin because we all have the same weaknesses, but now we have a King who has overcome sin. In Jesus, God has led a sinless life for us in a body of the same carnal nature that we have and offers forgiveness to all who will sincerely acknowledge Him.

When you think about all the hateful evil that the devil inspired the ones who were supposed to be the keepers of God's laws on earth to commit against Him from His arrest to His death on the cross, you have to realize that we are saved by the skin of our teeth and deserve no mercy. Motivated by paranoid fear of the things that the devil established to rule this world, they would not trust Jesus because He came simply affirming and explaining God's laws, and while they may have really believed that a messiah would come, they would not trust Jesus with no army. They could only perceive that Satan could only be overcome by beating him at his own game.

They knew that what they were doing was not right but were so intensely afraid that the people who believed in Him would rise up in the only way they could imagine that they were afraid to treat Him justly.

They were afraid to trust God because Satan rules the world with fear; fear that you can't trust and follow God because Satan's power to keep the world in fear will over-come and destroy us if we resist. In their case it was fear of the power of the Roman government.

This fear of the power of Satan to keep us captive caused the High Priest, Caiaphas, to utter some of the most weirdly profound prophetic words in all of history, "Better that one man should perish than the whole nation." (John 11:49-51)

God knew what He was doing when He made us. He fully understood the incredible power of Satan to deceive, and He took in advance the responsibility of providing what we need to overcome Satan and his deceptions. He knew that Satan would waste no time corrupting His creation. That is why He made us the way He did, to live first in our carnal nature.

Because of this, every one of us has fallen to sin. We do not really have the power to save ourselves and could only look forward to the everlasting corruption of strife and misery that Satan would lead us to were it not that, in Jesus, God has provided the way of escape.

It is far more than just an escape. When we come to Jesus, we are coming home. Like a lost child in a big scary world who was found and brought home, we are safe at last. We're still in that big scary world but now we know that we are where we belong, where we're loved, and with those who will make our future secure.

God knows that we have to be exposed to both good and evil if we're going to know the difference and we must come to the determination to choose the good of our own free will. That is why He brought us into being with the nature we have now first and that is why He was, in Christ, willing before creation, to suffer the agony of the cross. He loves us that much.

To understand Jesus, you have to understand Him in the spiritual sense, that He was involved in our creation, and in charge of our development into what He intended us to be from the start. You must also understand that you were made to be of free will spiritually; able to reject His spirit if you choose.

The choice that you are making is this: You are acknowledging that what you are now is incapable of real righteousness and will die. You are now asking Jesus to lead you into His spiritual family where you belong, and you're agreeing to trust Him in this.

Chapter 6

What Jesus Does

You can't really be a Christian if you don't understand not only who Jesus is, but what He does and why He does things the way He does. Let me stress again that following Jesus is a choice. Every living soul will, at some point, have to choose or reject Him of his own volition. You can't be what God wants you to be if you are not a free spirit, like Himself, choosing to let Him conform you to maturity in the image of Christ. You have to decide and come to Him, and He will save you.

This involves two things. First, you must realize that, to God, righteousness is perfectly sincere righteousness. Jesus said that the most important commandment is to love The Lord your God with all your heart, and the second is to love your neighbor as yourself. We don't really do that. To do that in this world is impossible in our carnal nature with all the distraction that the devil carries on continually. It is literally impossible for us to overcome sin in our carnal state in this world. But we can come to Jesus in sincere acknowledgement of our sin. This is the first step, sincere confession and repentance.

The second thing is faith. If you don't have faith in Him, there is no sense in confessing your sin. He already knows that you are a sinner. If you believe that you are unable to overcome sin on your own, you are coming to Him because you believe that He can change you and your fate. We have now come to an area that can be confusing to some who are new to the faith. This doesn't mean that God is going to take complete control of you. The only thing that was ever predestined, in the sense that it was preset and unalterable, was that Christ would come, and that was because it was the will of God for something that He would do Himself.

When you come to Jesus in repentance, you are turning your life over to Him and your salvation is secure, but that is because you are now in a new relationship.

If God is going to bring forth sons and daughters by taking control so that we can only think and act however He wants, there is certainly little purpose in suffering and dying for us, and it would bring no satisfaction that we would love Him. You're not preprogrammed robots; You're the sons and daughters of a wonderful Father who loves you with the sincerest love in the universe and wants to give you the best guidance possible.

God is fair. He makes His sun to shine on the just and unjust. If you were an unjust person who rejected Christ's influence in your life, you would think it unfair if you found out that He completely controlled the fate of those who accepted Him, which would give them an unearned advantage over you.

That is how He works in our lives; in the same way that a good father wants to provide guidance to his children, so that they build character and make wise choices in life. He wouldn't want to just make us be whatever He wanted us to be without the ability to choose.

Jesus has one big advantage over earthly fathers, though. He knows your every thought and the thoughts of everyone involved with you. As soon as you begin your new relationship with Him, He gives you the Holy Spirit that dwells within all who accept Him, and He will not abandon you, because He knows you and loves you.

Jesus is described as filling many roles in Bible prophesy. We have already noted that in the first prophesy in Genesis, God would allow the devil to work, but the seed of the woman would defeat him. Much Bible prophesy describes Him in his kingly role as the One who would finally throw the devil out and rule the world in righteousness. The second Psalm is about the second coming and describes Him as God's appointed king who will come in victory when the ruling forces of this world are set for the final blow to destroy His people and the worship of God on earth.

> Why do the nations rage, and the peoples imagine a vain thing?
> The kings of the earth set themselves, and the rulers take counsel together, against the Lord, and against His anointed, saying,
> Let us break their bands asunder and cast away their cords from us.
> He who sitteth in the heavens shall laugh; The Lord shall have them in derision.

Then shall He speak to them in His wrath and vex them in His great displeasure. Yet have I set my king upon my holy hill of Zion.

I will declare the decree; The Lord said unto me, thou art my son; this day have I begotten thee.

Ask of me and I will give thee the nations for thine inheritance, and the uttermost parts of the earth for thy possession.

Thou shalt break them with a rod of iron; thou shalt dash them in pieces like a potter's vessel.

Be wise now, therefore, O ye kings; be instructed ye judges of the earth.

Serve the Lord with fear and rejoice with trembling.

Kiss the son, lest he be angry, and ye perish from the way, when his wrath is kindled but a little. Blessed are they who put their trust in him. (Psalm 2)

The prophets describe him as a king who will govern the earth in an orderly manner that, unlike everything that preceded his reign, works, resulting in permanent peace and prosperity. Isaiah says this in chapter 9,

For to us a child is born, unto us a son is given, and the government shall be upon his shoulders; and his name shall be called Wonderful, Counselor, The mighty God, The everlasting Father, The Prince of Peace.

> Of the increase of His government there shall
> be no end, upon the throne of David, and
> upon His kingdom, to order it, and to estab-
> lish it with righteousness from henceforth
> even forever. The zeal of the Lord of hosts
> will perform this. (Isaiah 9:6)

"To us a child is born" clearly shows that Jesus can be thought of as one of us, having fully experienced life as a man, but He is also called the "Mighty God," and "The everlasting Father." The success of His reign comes because of the power of God, "The zeal of the Lord of hosts will perform this."

When David expressed the desire to Nathan the prophet to build a house for the Lord, Nathan first told David to do what was in his heart, but later that night, the word of the Lord came to him to tell David that the Lord would build him a house.

"And when thy days be fulfilled and thou shalt sleep with thy fathers, I will set up thy seed after thee, which shall proceed out of thine own body, and I will establish his kingdom. He shall build an house for my name, and I will establish the throne of his kingdom forever." (2 Samuel 7:12,13)

The last recorded words of David were these,

> The spirit of the Lord spoke by me, and
> his word was in my tongue. The God of Israel
> said, the Rock of Israel spoke to me, He who
> ruleth over men must be just, ruling in the
> fear of God. And he shall be as the light of the
> morning, when the sun riseth, even a morning

without clouds, and as the tender grass sprin-
geth out of the earth by clear shining after rain.

Although my house is not so with God,
yet he hath made with me an everlasting covenant, ordered in all things, and sure; for
this is all my salvation, and all my desire,
although he maketh it not to grow.

But the sons of Belial shall be all of them
as thorns thrust away, because they cannot
be taken with hands. But the man who
shall touch them must be armed with iron
and the staff of a spear; and they shall be
utterly burned with fire in the same place.
(2 Samuel 23:2-7)

The Lord promised David that he would be the ancestor
of Christ, that Christ would overcome the works of the
devil, which earthly rulers could not do, because He was
armed with the power of God. The sons of Belial cannot
be taken by hands, it can only be done with God's spirit.

The fullness of what Jesus does couldn't really be understood until after He came and finished the work of His first
coming on earth. He would experience everything that we
do, including birth, life, death, and then resurrection into
a new spiritual body and life in that state.

In the Bible we have the first four gospels, Matthew,
Mark, Luke, and John, and next the Acts of the Apostles.
Luke wrote both Luke and Acts. It may help you to under-
stand more completely to read the two together.

At the end of Luke, the risen Christ appears to the
eleven disciples as they were gathered in Jerusalem.

> And as they thus spoke, Jesus himself
> stood in the midst of them, and saith unto
> them, Peace be unto you. But they were ter-
> rified and frightened and supposed that they
> had seen a spirit.
>
> And he said unto them, why are ye trou-
> bled? And why do thoughts arise in your
> hearts? Behold my hands and feet, that is
> I myself; handle me, and see; for a spirit
> hath not flesh and bones, as ye see me have.
> (Luke 24:38-39)

Jesus, now the firstborn among many brethren, appears
out of nowhere, but He is not just a spirit; He has a real
body and invites them to touch Him so that they will believe
Him. Next, He asked them if they had anything to eat, and
ate a piece of broiled fish and some honeycomb. "And He
said unto them, these are the words I spoke unto you, while
I was yet with you, that all things must be fulfilled, which
were written in the law of Moses, and in the prophets, and
in the Psalms, concerning me." (Luke 24:44)

The theme of the Old Testament, while it contains a lot
of history and wisdom literature, is the coming of Christ
and is authored by Him through inspiration.

> Then he opened their understanding,
> that they might understand the scriptures,
> and said unto them, thus it is written and
> thus it behooved Christ to suffer, and to
> rise from the dead the third day; and that
> repentance and remission of sins should

be preached in his name among all nations, beginning at Jerusalem. And ye are witnesses of these things.

And behold, I send the promise of my father upon you; but tarry ye in the city of Jerusalem, until ye be endued with power from on high. (Luke 24-49)

Here, He spoke of the Holy Spirit:

And he led them out as far as Bethany; and he lifted up his hands and blessed them. And it came to pass, while he blessed them, that he was parted from them, and carried up into heaven.

And they worshiped him and returned to Jerusalem with great joy; and were continually in the temple, praising and blessing God. Amen.(Luke 24: 50-53)

This is the end of Luke's gospel. He next begins the Acts of the Apostles, "The former treatise have I made, O Theophilus, of all that Jesus began to do and to teach."

The earthly appearance of Jesus, His ministry, and His resurrected appearance to some on earth, then, is just simply described as the beginning of His work.

"Until the day in which he was taken up after he, through the Holy Spirit, had given commandments unto the apostles whom he had chosen. To whom he also showed himself alive after his passion by many infallible proofs, being seen by them forty days, and speaking of the things pertaining to the kingdom of God; and being assembled together with them, commanded that they should not depart from Jerusalem, but wait for the promise of the Father, which saith he, ye have heard from me.

For John truly baptized with water; but ye shall be baptized with the Holy Spirit not many days from now."

It is very clear that even the disciples who had been with Him still did not yet understand the spiritual nature of what He was going to do. They then asked Him if He would at that time restore the kingdom to Israel.

Jesus replied, "It is not for you to know the times or the seasons, which the Father hath put in his own power. But ye shall receive power after the Holy Spirit is come upon you; and ye shall be witnesses unto me, both in Jerusalem, and in Judea, and in Samaria and unto the uttermost parts of the earth." (Acts 1:2-8)

Then Jesus was taken up out of their sight and as they stood gazing up, two men in white apparel stood by them and said, "Ye men of Galilee, why stand ye gazing up into heaven? This same Jesus, who is taken up from you into heaven, shall come in like manner as ye have seen Him go up into heaven." (Acts 1:11

What Jesus was beginning to do through the Holy Spirit was a new concept to the disciples. They were all thinking of the Messiah as simply one who would come as a king who would establish Israel as the nation ruling the whole world and forcing everyone to conform to the Mosaic law. Jesus will come as a conquering king when the time comes but the most important of His works was just beginning. All else would be in vain without His work through the Holy Spirit.

Paul says in First Corinthians 15:50 that "flesh and blood cannot inherit the kingdom of God; neither doeth corruption inherit incorruption." The kind of kingdom that the apostles envisioned is neither satisfactory to God nor even possible for carnal mankind.

Remember the zeal and courage of Peter. Peter really believed in Jesus and reverenced Him, but when Jesus began to tell the disciples what would happen to Him when they went to Jerusalem, that He would have to suffer and die for them, Peter could not accept this and took Him aside, rebuking Him and insisting that this would not be.

Before they came to arrest Jesus in the garden Peter had felt sure of his full commitment to Him. When Jesus had said that He was going somewhere that they could not follow, Peter had asked, "Why can I not follow you now? I will lay down my life for you," but Jesus then told him that before the cock crowed, he would deny him three times. (Luke 22: 33-34)

When they came to arrest Jesus, Peter was gung-ho to draw swords and fight it out, but Jesus would not allow it, telling him to put up his sword. In the following hours Peter probably experienced about as much tribulation, anxiety, and uncertainty as anyone ever does. He still had the courage to follow with John to see what would happen next.

He wanted to be able to do something but could only be there and watch, feeling completely helpless and useless. When some of the staff asked him if he were not one of the disciples, he said he was not, just wanting to be left alone to watch. Later when they asked again, he said not, and when they began to insist that he was, with impatient anger he cursed and swore that he didn't know the man. The cock crowed.

Jesus then turned and looked at him and bold Peter went out and wept bitterly. I believe at that moment Peter fully saw Jesus and knew that his precious Lord had to suffer and die for his sins. I can only imagine the anguish of soul, self-condemnation, and the helplessness that he felt. He felt himself not fit as an apostle and undeserving of the love of Jesus.

Jesus knew this and knew Peter better than Peter knew himself. When Mary and Mary Magdalene went to His tomb the angels told them to go and tell the others, "and Peter," that He was risen. Jesus was fully aware of what Peter was going through. Having now lived as a man in our state, He is sympathetic to us in every challenge that we face and is willing to help when we ask in trust.

But with His death and resurrection, He entered into a new role. He is now the risen, fully justified King in charge of the whole earth. Now raised in a different eternal body, He began His work of rebirth and preparation for spiritual resurrection for believers. But we are all like Peter. No one in this carnal body we now have could be more well intentioned than he was, but like him, we will all fail on our own spirituality. We need help and we need not to be held fully accountable if we are to be changed.

Jesus does this through the Holy Spirit. When He appeared to the disciples, He instructed them not to begin the work of evangelizing until they had received Him. None of us can accomplish spiritual things under our own power.

The Holy Spirit, like Jesus Himself, is part of God. God sends the Holy Spirit to everyone who comes to trust Jesus as Lord and Savior. He resides within you as a guide and counselor. He prepares you for your change when the work is finished. As long as you live in this carnal body, you still have the nature of sin, but that is forgiven, and God accepts you because of your relationship with Christ. All you have to do is be open and sincere with Jesus, trust Him, accept His lordship over your life, and keep practicing on that relationship, and He will bring you through to something that is too wonderful for you to even imagine now.

That is what Jesus does. He is your personal advocate with God, providing all you need to transform yourself from the old carnal nature to the new nature of the Son of God, giving you rebirth through the Holy Spirit that He puts within you.

Chapter 7

Who Are You?

The Bible says that you are a special creation of God, made in His own image, and if you are not that, then nothing that Jesus has done makes any sense. If you are that, then Jesus is the most important thing in the world to you.

One of the greatest challenges that a young person who is not well versed in the Bible faces today is the universal teaching that mankind evolved from lower life forms into what we are now. In the present secular culture, the evolution of man is usually spoken of as a proven fact, assuming that everyone accepts and acknowledges it. We are all familiar with hearing about how various aspects of our anatomy can be explained in terms of how we evolved.

But did we evolve or were we designed to be this way. The Bible doesn't say that no species have experienced any changes in the earth's history, but it does say that man was a specific creation of God.

In school we were taught that we evolved from more primitive creatures, and if you were taking a test that required an answer to affirm that hypothesis, you would be counted wrong if you didn't.

The basis for this is that the study of fossil evidence indicates that animal life forms have undergone changes throughout earth's history. Darwin theorized that changes occur because of mutations and the natural selection of the fittest to meet environmental changes. If fossil evidence indicates that other species have undergone physical changes through the ages, then mankind must have also undergone physical changes over time. The finding of fossils of creatures manlike in form is taken as proof of our evolution.

But think back to the beginning of life on earth. I doubt that modern science would disagree with the description of earth as it was given in Genesis, that in the beginning it was not a solid form but rather more of a nebulous nature and eventually came to solidify with the surface becoming land and water. I think that science would say that the first life forms to appear would have been simple, one-celled organisms.

What caused that to evolve into giant dinosaurs and other prehistoric animals? How would trillions of cells come together to form an animal? How did the method of sustenance and propagation become so different? It seems that sustenance and propagation would have followed a pattern of evolution derived from improvements in the original form; that is, splitting and absorption. But instead, we find multitudes of different types of cells put together, not independently sustaining themselves, but organized into a sort of machine.

We eat and we drink. We have saliva glands to prepare food for digestion. We have mouths and teeth to grind it.

We have muscles that swallow food into a tube that leads to the stomach. The stomach secretes fluids that are strong enough to digest the food, but it is made of cells that are unharmed while it does it. From there the food is carried into another tube at the right time and then into the blood vessels, another series of smaller tubes, where nourishment is carried all over the body. Somehow this is distributed in the exact quantities needed to nourish or store and regenerate the many different types of tissues that make up the body every day throughout our lifetimes.

Everywhere, you find highly specialized organs and tubes that perform specific purposes. The heart continually pumps blood into the circulatory system, the lungs continually breathe air in and out, providing oxygen, and eliminating carbon dioxide. There are special organs that filter and eliminate excess liquid and waste. The body can move because of a network of nerves that connect to the brain and instantly transmit signals. The brain controls the whole body. It sees through the eyes, hears through the ears, tastes, feels, and smells through the nerve connections, and it thinks, reasons, remembers, balances, and moves muscles.

When you think about it, the body is a complicated machine, actually controlled by the most sophisticated computer system ever devised. With so many parts and different types of tissues working in conjunction, it is absurd to think that this just sprang up and evolved on its own. All your vital parts had to have been created at the same time because no one part can live without the others.

Picture the development of animal life and try to reconcile it with evolution. At what point did a brain appear to control all the bodily functions? Was the nervous system already there? Did the circulatory system appear before or after the heart? How did a pulmonary and circulatory system appear and evolve when the body can only live moments without them working? Your eyes and ears are highly specialized organs that no mammal can effectively function without. How long did it take them to evolve? How did a heart that beats continually begin? When did teeth develop? Was the stomach already there and if so, why? When did the metabolic process of keeping the body, a certain temperature begin?

In this world, where our subliminal thoughts are so conditioned by secularism, we tend to automatically bypass reason and think that if we assign enough millions of years to it that those things could have just slowly developed on their own. But when you think it through, you realize that animal life could not be the result of a series of slow steps. Creation by God of the diversity of life we see in the world around us is the only real possibility, and if some evolution occurred it is because it was created with the ability to do that.

The Bible says that, when God created animal life, He created them male and female. That is another reason why we could not have evolved. Two types are required to reproduce, and they had to have been created at the same time. They have two different types of organs and glands, with the female designed to conceive, bear, and nurture new life, and the male to impregnate. Both have their different hormonal systems that cause them to be different physically and emotionally.

Here, in the hormonal system, we have compelling evidence of design rather than evolution. All of our bodily functions, even our emotions, are controlled by hormones. Hormones are special chemicals that act as messengers, stimulants, and regulators to every operation of the body. Each type of hormone is secreted by a particular gland specifically designed to produce it in the right amounts when needed.

Some, such as adrenalin, act in response to sudden, sporadic needs, increasing the oxygen supply to the muscles, heart, and lungs in reaction to fear. Some are active continually, and others are activated during certain stages of life and switch on or off automatically. There are hormones that control growth, causing you to grow in childhood and ceasing to grow at adulthood. Hormones cause you to mature sexually at puberty. There are hormones that stimulate contractions in childbirth and others that cause the production of milk in the mammary glands for a period after birth occurs. They enable you to digest food, resist disease, sleep, and rebuild every component of the body.

Hormones cause you to feel the way you do when you experience all your emotions: love, hate, anger, sorrow, fondness, boredom, interest, fear, and comfort. Your thoughts cause a chemical reaction so that all of these are poignantly "felt." The mind's connection to the hormonal system to enable us to feel such a wide variety of emotions sets us apart from the other animals. Your dog experiences fear in danger or the comfort of being with those he is fond of, but the hormonal circuit board for our emotional experience is much more intricate. We are designed to think and feel as God does.

There are some things about us that are different from all the other animals. We are equipped at creation to "subdue" the earth. We were meant to make the earth work for us. All other animals are assigned a territory and food source, and the "dread" of man is put into them, as the Bible says. We were created like we are. Looking back at history, there is no evidence of change from apelike creatures into modern man. In all of the history we can find of ourselves, mankind has worn clothes, had no more hair than now, built things, raised crops, talked and continued to increase. There are now several billions of us.

It is obvious that God made us different from all others and intended for us to increase from the beginning. When God made a mate for Adam, He made her with some differences from the way females were designed in the other animals. Not only were women designed to be far more attractive to the sexual appetite of men, but also the two sexes were made to have a unique emotional and spiritual need for each other.

Male deer have antlers, male lions have manes, and a few other animals have such distinguishing features, but nowhere in the animal kingdom is found as much difference in physical structure or natural conduct as between man and woman.

The softness of her skin, beauty of her face, placement of fat on her body, graceful movement, soft voice, and gentle touch were all designed by God to make woman the perfect mate for man. Women didn't evolve this way because they stayed in the cave and tended the fire while the men went out to hunt mastodons. They were made like they are so that God's plan would work. He designed our physical and emotional natures, both men and women, so that we could best complete the purpose for which we were made.

Now we come to the greatest difference between us and the other animals. When God made Adam, He breathed into him the breath of life. You are not just an advanced animal species. God has put within you the seed of His spiritual nature. He didn't just make us with strong sexual attraction to fill the earth. Every physical body created will die.

God has provided guidance for us to steer us through life in this physical body so that we can enjoy our physical nature and nurture the spiritual; and it is basically a matter of putting the spiritual first. God intended for a man and woman to live together in a unique bond, faithful and devoted to each other, so that they would love and respond to each other. He intended that they would nourish a sense of belonging and purpose from that, being strengthened and growing in wisdom, so that it would be easier to follow the way of the spirit and establish that as tradition.

You were designed, and by your Creator; you were designed for a purpose. That purpose is spiritual, but your journey to fullness begins in an animal body. Your body is really just temporary housing, and your brain, with its unique connection to your hormonal system is actually just the command center for the human "machine" that your body is. In a sense it is just a form of "artificial intelligence." You were designed to ultimately live in a spiritual body in communion with God as part of His family.

There is a good reason why God made you to live first with a nascent spirit nature in a carnal body. Both the carnal and the spiritual can be corrupted; but it is much easier to corrupt the carnal.

When Adam and Eve disobeyed God in Eden, they hid themselves in the trees and God called them. Now God already saw them and knew where they were and what they had done. But Adam and Eve had hoped that they could hide themselves, being now aware of their nakedness, and hoped to be able to deceive God into thinking that He had not seen what He certainly saw. They couldn't "see" everything like God does, and they were aware that, even though they had a likeness to Him, there was something superior about Him. To admit the truth to Him would have been an admission of their own lack of His perfection and it wounded their pride. Something or someone besides themselves had to be blamed.

This is an inextricable part of the carnal nature of man. We all have an innate, subliminal perception that there is another nature, higher than ours, from which the truth cannot be hidden or distorted. We all know that that is the nature of the One who made us, and we all know, no matter how suppressed that knowledge may be, that we are all subject to Him like children to a father. The carnal reaction is a feeling of frustrated resentment and denial.

When God looks at us, He sees clearly our innermost thoughts. When we try to perceive the unsaid by others, we apply the science of knowing our own nature. We always look for the control of the carnal nature, not the spiritual, and are usually right. This is true in both grave matters and trivial. And whether we be the analyzed or the analyst, the judged or the judge, we are all unable to really detach ourselves from that carnal nature. Every Christian knows that we should be like God, but we'll never come up to that standard. Even though we understand why we should, we are unable. This is true of you and me, and with Adam, with Moses, the apostles, and every great evangelist and religious thinker who ever lived.

If you come to realize that this world is full of turmoil, distrust, injustice, and strife because of our nature and ask why can't I have the mindset of God and be different, the honest answer is that you can't. It has been this way from the moment when the devil planted the first seed of doubt in the mind of Eve, and no one has overcome it. Our carnal nature prevails.

I believe that God created us in this condition for a very good reason. If He were just going to abandon us until we straighten up and fly right, it would be another matter, because He well knew our weakness, but that is not what He did. He never intended us to live on in this nature. Our bodies will die. But He has put within us another nature, and it is a latent nature until He enlivens it: a spirit man, which is what we can look forward to being, has a more god-like ability to "see," and perceive thoughts. Such a creature needs to be free from the carnal desires and nature that limits us now. If the devil were going to deceive and corrupt such a creature, his best chance would be as soon as possible after that creature came into existence, when he was in the spiritually equivalent stage of Adam and Eve as carnal creatures in Eden.

Otherwise, each man would need to be created with a built-in resistance put into his mind. But God *is* making you after His own image, fully free to think for yourself. The kingdom of heaven is a totally honest and sincere kingdom of the children of God, the kingdom of perfect faith.

So, instead of just creating you as a "babe in the woods" but fully developed spirit man, He creates you as a carnal man with a latent spirit within. This spirit man comes alive by hearing the voice of the Son of God.

This change involves a conscious decision and commitment. When you come to Him in response, acknowledge that you are a sinner, and repent, He puts the Holy Spirit within you and your spiritual rebirth begins. When your spiritual development is complete, all that you have experienced in your life in this carnal state you will have experienced as a developing spirit person, under the Fatherhood and guidance of God through Jesus Christ and the Holy Spirit.

This is who you are, and God, through Jesus Christ, has provided all you need for eternal fulfillment and peace of mind. He has paid a dear price that none of us could pay ourselves so that you may have it. He did it because He knew that it was the only way, and He was willing to do it for you.

That Jesus has lived as one of us and He gave His life for us; suffering the agony of death on a cross is not a thing to be taken lightly. Everyone who hears of this needs to make a choice.

If you believe these things, the only wise choice is to follow Him. That is the first choice, and if you believe that you just evolved from a lower life form and when you die that is the end of you, then what?

Chapter 8

The Deceiver

A t first glance, it certainly seems that most Americans are choosing the second view. A fewer percentage than ever now attend church or tithe faithfully. Few are per- sistently making Bible study, prayer, and a personal rela- tionship with Christ their main motivation in life. We have become a far more secular people and a lot of people who do attend church would not consider that a binding and committed part of their lives.

On the other hand, I don't think you would find most of the people are really atheists. There is something about us that really seems to believe that we will live on after death. But the prevailing attitude is that this just happens and, if we are not egregious in our misconduct, there's nothing to worry about.

America was the most fertile ground for the great reli- gious revival that began in the 1700s and was still alive and vibrant in the first half of the 1900s. Christians in that era felt a deep sense of personal commitment to the Savior who gave His life for them, and it made a difference in the way they thought and acted, but this has been just about wiped out in the last sixty years or so.

Why has this happened? It is because many in the church have been deceived by the devil.

The message of the Bible is close-up and personal. Nowhere is it ever suggested that it is an abstract message. It is God speaking to you, telling you things that are true and outlining standards of conduct which, if a nation of people followed, they would eliminate most of the problems that now beset America. It is a personal relationship through adoption.

The devil doesn't win you over to his way by persuasive argument that you will be better off going to hell with him. All he needs to do is create a seed of doubt in your mind that what God says is true. If he can convince people that we just evolved from a lower life form, it creates doubt about everything the Bible says. The foundation outlined in the beginning of the Bible is not literally true, so, none of it can be taken as literal truth. You no longer really have a God who created you for a clear purpose, so you have to create your own purpose, if you want one, and your own code of conduct. Some sort of a god may be out there somewhere, but he is much farther away and not really involved with you in the fatherly sense.

The difference between Christ and the devil is this: Christ clearly identifies Himself as the One who created us, deeply loves us, and wants to guide us in the way that leads to eternal blessing. The devil never identifies himself but only seeks to deceive you and lead you away from Christ.

I am not an expert on the devil, or his motives and I don't think that any man really could be. He is described in the Bible as a spiritual being, a fallen angel, who always opposes God and wants to be like God himself.

Isaiah 14 speaks of him at the second coming of Christ,

> How art thou fallen from heaven, O Lucifer, son of the morning! How art thou cut down to the ground, which did weaken the nations!
>
> For thou hast said in thine heart, I will ascend into heaven, I will exalt my throne above the stars of God; I will sit also upon the mount of the congregation, in the sides of the north; I will ascend above the heights of the clouds; I will be like the most high.
>
> Yet thou shalt be brought down to hell, to the sides of the pit. They that see thee shall narrowly look upon thee, and consider thee, saying, is this the man that made the earth to tremble, that did shake the kingdoms? (Isaiah 14:12–16)

The devil is real. Paul says in Ephesians 6:10–12, "Finally my brethren, be strong in the Lord, that you may be able to stand against the wiles of the devil. For we wrestle not against the flesh and blood, but against principalities, against powers, against the rulers of the darkness of this world, against spiritual wickedness in high places."

Every Christian needs to know and understand the powers of the devil to deceive and corrupt us. To understand the devil, you must think of him in the same way that

I said earlier that you must think of Christ. Don't diminish him to one of your own limitations. He sees a lot farther than you can.

Like a general and his staff in his headquarters in a war, in a room full of maps showing the position of his troops and the enemy, checking the weaknesses and strengths of both, watching supply lines, constantly monitoring reconnaissance reports, and anticipating possible moves, he has a plan and an agenda to destroy our faith in Christ.

In this day of instant communication, organized schools of worldly thought, educational systems, news reporting, cultural influence from television, movies, literature, and more, he knows how to proceed strategically, systematically, and effectively with every tool. He's not just out there throwing darts, helter-skelter, at individual Christians, but following a well-orchestrated plan.

In Paul's day, the devil was well-aware of the prevailing culture of the time and tried to use it in every way, from either subverting Christian thought within the church to turning external forces against them.

The Greco-Roman culture of the time was, in many ways, like the present in America. The Roman Empire was a conglomeration of cultures and creeds brought together with powerful secular influence. Few people took seriously the old religions and idols anymore. It had become a secular world, seeking something, and knowing not what, ripe for the devil's confusing and perversive influence.

In Acts 17:21, leading up to Paul's sermon on Mars Hill, he gives us a picture that is a good description of the gentile world at that time, "For all the Athenians and strangers who were there spent their time in nothing else, but to hear or tell some new thing." They were interested in religious ideas, but of course, not drawn by any spiritual conviction. Their main motivation was fascination with secular human wisdom.

With such a wide panoply to draw from, the devil found it easy to bring divisive and destructive elements into the new church. Not being led by the Holy Spirit, they had an interest in the new Christian faith, but wanted to come in pursuing their own ideas of wisdom, bringing in heresies that were off course from the provision of the Holy Spirit.

The early church had to deal with sects that propounded such ideas as that Christ never really died on the cross, being a spirit who was immune to human suffering, or that our conduct didn't matter because we would be changed anyway. The only way to avoid being trapped in such deceptions is to have a clear conception of who Jesus is and a deep commitment to live in a relationship with Him. If you are drawn to Him in this simple, deeply personal way, you will be motivated to think and act according to His will and you will want to publicly honor Him in regular assembly with others who share the same drawing. The longer you live with this commitment, the more you will understand and treasure what He is doing for you.

The apostles and early leaders of the church were aware of the dangers of false doctrine creeping in and vehemently insisted that the fundamentals of the faith had to be taken literally and their relationship with Christ personally.

Peter, in his second letter1:16 through 2:1 said

> For we have not followed cunningly
> devised fables when we made known to you

the power and coming of our Lord Jesus Christ but were eyewitnesses to his majesty.

For he received from God the Father, honor and glory, when there came such a voice to him from the excellent glory, this is my beloved Son, in whom I am well pleased. And this voice, which came from heaven, we heard, when we were with him in the holy mount.

We also have a surer word of prophecy, unto which ye do well that ye should take heed, as a light that shineth in a dark place, until the day dawn, and the day star arise in your hearts. Knowing this first, that no prophesy of the scripture is of any private interpretation (that is, not isolated from what the scriptures say altogether). For the prophecy came not at any time by the will of man, but holy men of God as they were moved by the Holy Spirit.

But there were false prophets among the people, even as there shall be false teachers among you, who secretly shall bring in destructive heresies, even denying the Lord that bought them, and bring upon them-selves swift destruction.

It is very important that you always keep to the funda-mentals of the faith. This attempt to bring in false doctrines to weaken the faith has always gone on. The difference in how effective it has been through the ages is how focused the people in the church were on the things that Peter and the early church leaders outlined in their day to combat it.

Many Christians of my age are now appalled when we look back at how the church has declined in power and see how close the devil is coming to being able to outlaw the final remnants. If we are ever going to give this nation the wake-up call that will be effective, we're going to have to first get a clear picture of the long-range strategy that the enemy has been following. These things don't happen overnight. It took many years of massive, well-orchestrated schemes to get and keep us so distracted from the fundamentals of the faith that he could wreak this much damage and decline.

Clearly understanding the methods of the enemy, we're going to have to be following a defined course of action to defeat him and bring us back to Christ in revival. This can only be done with the leadership of the Holy Spirit. We cannot accomplish anything in a spirit of panic or fear, or with our own zeal.

Jesus said, "Abide in me and I in you, As the branch cannot bear fruit of itself, except it abide in the vine, no more can ye, except ye abide in me." (John 15:4)

If the churches in America that have been deceived by Satan will turn to Jesus in faith, discard their man-made gospels, and trust the Holy Spirit to be their voice, He will lead us into a great revival.

Chapter 9

Preparing for Revival

When Jesus came to earth to live as a man, He did it as one of us. The only powers above ours that He used were some acts of kindness toward others in healing. In walking His own personal path, He did so under the same challenges that we do.

That includes not being able, by divine fiat, to stop your enemies from lying about you, twisting your words, or trying to create false impressions about what you do or say. The devil was not put under some sort of divine gag order so that only the truth could be spoken about Him, and this was true then and it is true now.

Just as you must live in a carnal body with a latent spirit, with the devil ceaselessly trying to deceive and corrupt you, so did He. He did what He was sent to do, and now He operates under the divine authority, of whom He is part, as the Son, to lead you through, as the first born among many brothers.

Reflect on that for a moment!

Jesus has taken on, not just all the enemy had to throw at Him in His own earthly life, but after that, the same for each of us who come to Him. There is a relentless spiritual war going on in the world and the weapons used are deception and truth. It has to be this way because God made you to be like Him by choice, not as a robot.

Jesus has already done everything that can be done for you, even dying on a cross. It will not do you any good if you don't take the next step, surrendering your life to Him. If you were important enough to Him to do that for you, do you not owe it to Him to try to persuade others to come to Him? He didn't do it just for you.

In this fight, Jesus is still playing by the same rules that He did before. If you were running for political office, you'd want to swing the way things are done in a certain direction. You also know that in order to win, you need to have as many voters as possible convinced that your way is the best way, and you need to have them talking it up to persuade others. You also need them to show up on election day. You owe it to Jesus to support Him.

To do that, you need to be convinced yourself that Jesus and what the Bible says about Him is real. Do the things that I've said make sense to you? If they do, then you also need to know why you can believe that they are based on historical fact; is the Bible reliable from the standpoint of historical accuracy? It is!

In this spiritual war that is being waged, Jesus knows that we need to hear the truth to believe it. Despite all the devil can do to blind us to it, He has given us the truth and preserved it in the Bible.

Now, the men who wrote the Bible across a wide time span were not sitting there equipped with a recorder so that what they wrote was the exact transcript of what God spoke. The Holy Spirit came upon them and caused the thoughts that came into their minds. The Holy Spirit has always worked through stirring the spiritual part of carnal man. God has seen to it that the Bible contains His message to you so that, with the help of the Holy Spirit, you could understand and discern that it is true.

Looking at the Bible, we find that everything God said would happen already has, except the second coming of Christ and thereafter. What He spoke in Eden was true, what He said to Abraham came true, what Moses said about Him speaking through the great prophet came true; when God said that He would destroy and scatter the kingdom of Israel, not to return until the latter days, it came true. When He told Daniel in Babylon how long it would be before Messiah, it came true. When He revealed to Daniel the interpretation of Nebuchadnezzar's dream about a statue of a man and revealed the succession of the Babylonian, Persian, Greek, and Roman empires, and the emergence of the present political state of the world, it all came true. All we lack now is the final part of the dream when the image is struck on the toes with a stone, not cut with human hands and Christ's kingdom established. We have certainly reached the final part of this age.

Christ is the theme throughout the Bible. The prophets all spoke of him, both in His first advent and the next. The Messianic Psalms 2, 8, 16, 22, 23, 24, 40, 41, 45, 68, 69, 72, 89, 102, 110, and 118 are about Him. These Psalms clearly depict Him as God's anointed ruler who will bring wisdom and righteousness to the world. They show His humanity and His divinity. They poignantly describe how He would feel in agony on the cross. They reveal Him as having power over life and death. They tell us that His enemies will be destroyed and those who are faithful will be blessed eternally. Sometimes even small details of future events are revealed.

The Bible is true, and it was inspired by the Holy Spirit to lead you to Christ. The gospel that we want to bring to the world is real and the part that He wants you to play in spreading it begins with knowing Jesus yourself by the revelation of the Holy Spirit, acknowledging Him as your savior, and surrendering the work to Him in trust.

In the book of Revelation, Jesus tells John to "write the things thou hast seen, and the things which are, and the things which shall be hereafter." (Rev. 1:19) He then addresses seven churches, speaking to their angels.

In these messages to the churches in Asia, we can also see a depiction of the church in general from there to the end of the church age. The same concluding theme is found in the message to each church, similar to the first one, Ephesus. "He that hath an ear, let him hear what the spirit saith unto the churches; to him that overcometh will I give to eat of the tree of life, which is in the midst of the paradise of God." His salvation is always open to every individual.

The first church, Ephesus, characterizes the early church at the end of the apostolic age, commending their faith but warning against letting false doctrine come in.

The second church, Smyrna, is the church growing and facing persecution in the Roman world, and he commends them for resisting false doctrine and encourages them to stand firm in persecution.

The third, Pergamum, is the church under official acceptance. Here he warns against mixing the pure doctrines of the church with the things of the world, "Because thou hast there them that hold the doctrine of Balaam, who taught Balak to cast a stumbling block before the children of Israel, to eat things sacrificed to idols, and to commit fornication." (Rev 2:14)

The doctrine of Balaam refers to Balak, the Moabite king who tried to hire Balaam, whom he considered to be a holy man with magical spiritual influence, to curse the Israelites. When after three attempts, each time after waiting for the word of God, Balaam was clear that they could not be cursed, he then went about trying to encourage them to blend the two cultures and marry women of Moab.

The Bible is always clear that there are differences in the world and the church of God. You can't straddle the fence and be both, and the temptation to accept this became strong as soon as the church, having grown greatly, became officially accepted in the Roman Empire.

The fourth church, Thyatira, contained the same kind of warning, "Notwithstanding, I have a few things against thee, because thou allowest that woman, Jezebel, who calleth herself a prophetess, to teach and seduce my servants to commit fornication and to eat things sacrificed to idols." (Rev. 2:20)

The message here is the same. If you are not focused on Christ, the world will draw you into its web, and it did in the Middle Ages, but there were some who were true to Christ.

The fifth church, Sardis, represents the church that has mostly died. "I know thy works that thou hast a name that thou livest, and art dead." (Rev 3:1) Nevertheless, there were some who were true, and it was in this time that the reformation began.

The sixth church, Philadelphia, is addressed to the church during the great revival that began in the 1700s. To this church he says,

> "These things saith he that is holy, he that is true, he that hath the key of David, he that openeth and no man shutteth; and shutteth and no man openeth.
>
> I know thy works; behold, I have set before thee an open door, and no man can shut it; for thou hast a little strength, and hast kept my word, and hast not denied my name.
>
> Behold, I will make of the synagogue of Satan, who say they are Jews, and are not, but do lie; behold, I will make them to come and worship before thy feet, and to know that I have loved thee." (Rev. 7-9)

Now, pay particular attention to this next verse. "Because thou hast kept the word of my patience, I also will keep thee from the hour of temptation, which will come upon all the world, to try them that dwell upon the earth." (Rev. 3:10)

There is coming a time of great tribulation on earth that you want to avoid, if at all possible, and Jesus promised to keep them from it because of their faith.

Then He says,

> "Him that overcometh will I make a pillar in the temple of my God, and he shall go out

no more; and I will write upon hm the name of my God, and the name of the city of my God, the new Jerusalem, which cometh down out of heaven from my God; and I will write upon him my new name.

He that hath an ear, let him hear what the spirit saith to the churches." (Rev. 3:12-13)

The seventh and last church, Laodicea, is the church in its final state of apostacy. Jesus warned us in scripture that this would characterize the church at the end.

"And to the angel of the church of the Laodiceans write; These things saith the Amen, the faithful and true witness, the beginning of the creation of God. I know thy works, that they are neither cold nor hot; I would that thou wert cold or hot.

So then, because thou art lukewarm, I will spew thee out of my mouth. Because thou saith, I am rich, and increased with goods, and have need of nothing, and knowest not that thou are wretched, and poor, and blind and naked, I counsel thee to buy of me gold tried in the fire, that thou mayest be rich; and white raiment, that thou mayest be clothed, and that the shame of thy nakedness do not appear, and anoint thine eyes with salve, that thou mayest see.

As many as I love, I rebuke and chasten; be zealous, therefore, and repent.

Behold, I stand at the door and knock; if any man hear my voice, and open the door, I will come into him, and will sup with him, and he with me.

To him that overcometh will I grant to sit with me in my throne, even as I also overcame, and am sat down with my father in his throne.

He that hath an ear, let him hear what the spirit sayith to the churches.' (Rev. 3:14-22)

The Laodicean church is described as the lukewarm and apostate church but there is no reason to think that revival is not possible. Jesus gives the admonition to be zealous and repent. Clearly, we are in a time when the devil has worked a great corrupting deception in the church, but that doesn't mean that all hope is lost.

The same invitation to individual believers that is given in all the churches is given here too, but before that He says to the angel of the church to heed His counsel to realize that though we have more in worldly wealth, to open our eyes and see that we are poor spiritually.

Jesus is not telling us to hide in our shell and wait for the rapture; he wants us to revive and restore the church. "As many as I love, I rebuke and chasten. Be zealous, therefore, and repent."

To be zealous means to be ardently supportive of a cause, and to repent always means, not just to rue a past mistake, but to also change your course of action. There are more people now than there have ever been and more ways to communicate a message. Jesus wants as many as possible to hear the gospel and He wants it told by people who are believing and zealous for Him.

He has no need of a lukewarm church; He wants revival, and that can only come by the zealous effort of a people and church who clearly understand the things of Christ and what conflicting ways of the world have to be changed when we come to Him. God wants us to come to Him with the right motivation. Just as He came to us under our own human limitations, so should we be willing to work for Him with conviction and devotion in any environment, not just fear of the enemy. He will only revive us if we are willing to be what He wants us to be. Why would He want to restore power back to anything else?

If we want to see revival we need to get back to the kind of worship that preaches Christ under the power of the Holy Spirit. Get prepared by being what we are supposed to be, a people who love and trust Christ with deep personal conviction. If there is anything holding us back we need to take an honest look at it so we can understand it, repent, and be zealous. Nobody is going to get excited about Jesus if we aren't ourselves.

Chapter 10

What Happened

How have so many of us gone in such a short period of time from the Philadelphia church that Jesus so loved to the Laodicean church that He will spew because they are lukewarm?

Obviously, we need to sit down and take a good, long, hard look at the truth. We need to clearly see and understand the methods that Satan has used to corrupt us, and how commitment and faith in Christ could have prevented it and will bring us back in revival. We might as well know that if we let our minds go where Satan would direct our attention instead of where Jesus would lead us that he will make blind fools of us all.

The message in Revelation is to the church, not the nation. Jesus deals with the church. There are still many who are true to Jesus today, but they are increasingly the minority, and the time has come for the rest of the church to finally wake up, hear, and obey the voice of the Holy

Spirit. Otherwise, Jesus will spew you out to the power of the prince of this world.

Let's look at the way our nation has changed in just a few decades. Two things have shifted in a diametrical direction.

The thing that has most noticeably changed in the last sixty-five or, so years is the role of the family in our culture. In the 1950s, family was the cornerstone of our whole culture. The role of family was based on the belief in the sanctity of life. God made us to procreate and provided the way to do that, so that when we are created, we are provided with the atmosphere that forms character in us and gives the best chance of success. That provision is in marriage and earnestly striving to the best of our abilities as fathers and mothers to provide guidance to the children.

In the 1950s, not everyone got into an ideal marriage, and I suppose that there has never been a parent who was able to provide perfect guidance to the children, but you are certainly not going to do anything but worse if you're not trying! Back then divorce was a pretty rare thing; now it is common.

Now, everywhere you look, there are men and women living together, unwilling to commit to marriage, seeking only self-gratification, and trying to avoid the unwanted responsibility of children. Millions who were aborted never had a chance to be what they could have been. Our court system is now swamped with cases of child abuse, domestic violence, payment for child support, alimony, and other "family law" issues. We are taxed to support an army of social workers, psychologists, and lawyers to handle all of those things. Millions of children are in single parent homes and many of those are in homes provided by our taxes. You didn't see all this insanity when God was respected in America.

The breakdown of family began to deteriorate rapidly in the 1960s when birth control pills were invented and the temptation for premarital sex became greater than ever because the most immediate deterrent was almost eliminated.

Many young people went to seek their fortunes in the fastest growing areas of the country, and that weakened another constraint of sexual morality, the feeling of being known and identifiable in a familiar Christian culture. Many began to find themselves in a newly created culture where the sexual constraints of the old society were disappearing. Most still understood the good sense of the culture they came from where marriage was founded on the principle of a man and woman coming to know and trust that they would live committed to each other and take responsibility for any children that they had; but that was put on the back burner or tossed out the window, and satisfying the carnal appetite took over.

The next thing you know, more couples are beginning to live together unwed. When that happens, the old idea of commitment is gone, and the union is based strictly on whether the partner makes them feel that living together is "right." In other words, everything is now based on how self-serving it is, not commitment. No children are wanted while they make up their minds about each other.

The same generation begins to suffer the same reaction that Adam and Eve had when they disobeyed God in Eden. In spite of all, they still know that what they are doing is wrong. Some will try to justify it by claiming that it is logical in a world that has changed, but they still know that it is wrong.

They begin to fall away from the church and the faith because they no longer feel right about trying to act or talk like a Christian. They want to hide from God. Whereas they come from a generation where the parents of the children acted and spoke with authority to lead children in the right way, there is now an uncomfortableness that hampers that, and the devil is gaining ground quickly. He doesn't want to see the kind of strong Christian family life that we used to have in this country.

Now we come to the second thing that has shifted diametrically in America, the conceptual image that we have of our national culture. We no longer think of ourselves as being a Christian nation. That is also another thing that hampers the ability to lead children into the Christian faith. The media is so pervasive in our daily lives now that children cannot possibly be shielded from it and everything about it is designed to portray life in America as unapologetically and openly secular, sensual, and irreverent. There once was a time when a majority of the people could agree that freedom of speech meant the right to express political or moral opinions, not to flagrantly disregard basic prudence.

This nation desperately needs a great revival that will bring real repentance and zeal to every segment of our society. It is still possible to turn around and change our culture for the better, but I can promise you that any serious effort will be met with a swift and well-orchestrated counteroffensive of gigantic magnitude. The opposition is well-organized. The opposition we face today is a good example of how well-meaning people can be misled and corrupted by the devil when they try to improve worldly things by themselves and ignore God.

In the late 1800s a group of socialists in England formed and organization called the Fabian Society, named for a Roman general and statesman who employed guerilla tactics against Hannibal's forces and avoided open military confrontation. Their strategy for changing England to a socialist form of government was not to win voters over by persuasive argument that it was better, but rather to work within the existing system to change it one step at a time.

They sought to gain as much power and influence in the news media as possible, so that with each step, a powerful propaganda blitz could be provided to show a pressing and growing need for that particular element of socialism to be adopted into the capitalist system As this process went on people's subconscious perception would change to accept that government was supposed to operate under socialist principles.

Then, as now, the main activists and advocates of socialism were individuals who were born into wealth and privilege and considered themselves to be part of a highly intellectual group who were doing a good thing for the less fortunate masses who didn't have the capacity to understand that. They have had the means, influence, and time to build a powerful, international network out of this original seed that began with the Fabian Society. They now have a gargantuan amount of influence in many of the newspapers, television news agencies, talk shows, daily entertainment, movies, comedy, and drama shows that you are exposed to on a daily basis. They have also gained, probably, even more influence in institutions of higher learning, in how teachers are taught to teach, what goes into school textbooks, and even what aspiring preachers are taught in many seminaries about the Bible and how to preach. Every means of propaganda is now at their disposal to indoctrinate us to accept socialism.

I'm not implying that anything one might consider socialistic is wrong or that free enterprise is righteous, and socialism is evil. Free enterprise can lead to corruption as well as socialism. The Bible says that the "love of money" is the root of all evil, and there are some things that, as a matter of common sense, have to be done collectively, not of individual initiative. If people let the love of money control them in a free enterprise system, they will become depraved. The problem with modern socialist thinking is that the love of God is the root of all righteousness.

To understand the problems that they are creating, you need to look at the whole concept they have of what they think they are doing. They are not just trying to replace capitalism with socialism. They really see the ideal economic and social world more as "some form and degree" of socialism. In other words, socialism as an economic system is not perfected yet and it will require experimentation to get it to function best. The main goal right now is to inculcate you to accept the socialistic concept as the only appropriate way to think. They want you to equate that with righteousness and anything not in alignment as evil and radical.

Turning the United States into a socialist nation is only the secondary goal. The overall main goal is to bring the whole world together as a socialist world that will develop a one world government. This involves a long-term strategy.

Simply put, it is this; the destruction of cultural differences and religion and training us to think like one world socialists. The idea of the destruction of religion is a key element of socialism and the plan for that will be followed faithfully and systematically, regardless of what they tell you. They are fully confident that they will accomplish this eventually.

They envision a world like the one portrayed in the Star Trek television series where no one belongs to any group other that the worldwide secular culture and all religion is clearly understood to be a superstition that divided them in the past; a roadblock preventing enlightened minds from coming together in unity. Everyone seems to be perfectly content with his own assigned task, performing it to the best of his ability, and everyone has access to everything he wants. Socialism has never worked like that anywhere yet, but they still believe that we can be indoctrinated to make it work.

To see the orchestration with which they work is amazing to me. As far as I know, nothing more than what they would probably describe as an intellectual community exists. I do believe, personally, that because they believe that the communist system in China is the world's best candidate for transformation into the ideal they envision, that they have tried to work in sync with them in ways that have opened the door for a frightening amount of infiltration and influence. But they still operate like a well-oiled machine, in perfect cooperation. The effort to indoctrinate us by every propaganda instrument possible continues ceaselessly, and every planned attack, whether of an institution or an individual, is carried out with precise coordination. There is no regard for fair representation of any kind. As far as they are concerned, building this one world socialist society is always the greater good and the destruction of any ideological opposition is not subject to fair play.

You might think of the term "propaganda" only in the context of evil, but propaganda is something needed to bolster and preserve any ideology. God called on His people in the time of Moses and the law giving to actively maintain and proliferate a favorable outlook toward His precepts and the culture of people who worshipped Him.

Deuteronomy 6:6–7 says, "And these words, which I command thee this day, shall be in thine heart; And thou shalt teach them diligently unto thy children, and shalt talk of them when thou sittest in thine house, and when thou walkest by the way, and when thou liest down, and when thou risest up." This theme is found many times, throughout the Bible: that God's precepts must be publicly aired, taught, and expounded upon or it will be overwhelmed by worldliness.

The term *propaganda* comes from an early Christian organization, "The Propaganda Society." It was formed to spread a more favorable and understanding attitude at a time when many in the Roman Empire were hostile to the new Christian faith.

A good example of how propaganda can work in a more modern era can be seen in the way television sitcoms that involved family life were designed in the 1950s. Popular programs, such as "Leave It to Beaver" while showing in an amusing way, the natural inclination of young boys to get into mischief or confronted by the challenges we all face growing up, always portrayed parents as older, wiser, and taking responsibility for correction and guidance.

The unspoken moral had the good effect of making us feel that we live in a society where this manner of living is expected and held in approval. This concept of our society and the role we play in it is woven into the subconscious mind. It really has a lot more influence than we realize. That is especially true with young children and teenagers who all feel peer pressure. They want to feel like they fit in and are accepted by the group they're with and they identify the group as identifying with the popular culture of their perception.

If they perceive the society around them as one where most people are Christians and church goers, they accept that and are open to Christian precepts themselves. If they perceive society as non-churchgoing and indifferent or hostile toward religion, they will feel like being a Christian is a constraint that some are trying to force on them that will keep them from acceptance by the popular culture.

Socialist propaganda reflects the basic concept of socialism, that man is the product, and usually the victim of, his environment. It is almost never concerned with hyping the economic or social values of socialism, but rather, maligning the character and motives of any group or person seen as in opposition to their agenda, with the rightness of socialism assumed.

Christian propaganda hypes the value of individual strength and commitment to Christian principles. It is very effective in a culture that is already seen as Christian, but it takes more than propaganda to create and maintain a true Christian culture. The verse from Deuteronomy that I cited earlier says first that these words shall be in thine heart. This can only come from a commitment to a personal savior from the convincing of the Holy Spirit. If we don't have that, the corruption of worldliness will eventually win out. Christianity is not based on an idea; it is based on God, and we have to believe in Him and acknowledge Him. If we are not in subjection to the Holy Spirit and letting Him work, no amount of propaganda will turn us around.

Several years ago, I took a job doing some remodeling and restoration on an old house that was built in the 1800s that was being turned into a bed and breakfast. Before the anticipated opening date, the owner called one of the nearest T.V. stations to get the scheduled opening in the news.

I was in a room where the painters were working when they took some shots of Doug, who had been my painter and good personal friend for many years, doing some caulking. They had him to caulk down several corners until they could capture the best look of dogged determination on his face and forceful speed of movement that they wanted to show.

When they left the room, I laughed and kidded Doug about being the "lean, mean, caulking machine." Then I went to a roughed-in bathroom in another part of the house. The owner was in possession of some floor tile that he had bought a while back and didn't know where to find any more of it, so he wanted me to make sure there was enough of it before any installation. I was trying to determine a pattern that would make the least waste and see how many total pieces it would take.

I had put a piece of tile in a theoretical position, measured the distance from the wall, and sort of dropped my rule on the floor. Suddenly, I heard a voice telling me to throw my rule down with force. The next thing you know,

I was on the news as the resolute and dedicated flooring man, going at it hard and fast and determined to have it ready in time.

Every modern news reporter is trained in the art of using visual imagery to enhance viewer interest and sway emotion toward the desired influential effect. That is but one effective tool among many. If you can control enough news agencies today, you have a mind-boggling set of tricks in your arsenal for political propaganda.

To begin with, you're in charge of what's going to be news. Something that sounds negative about your opposition, though you may know it's not true, can be covered as a serious allegation and be all over the news day after day. The same sort of thing about your favored side, though there may be convincing evidence that it should be investigated, that can be ignored.

Of the multitudes of pictures of political figures taken daily, you can use the ones that, in a brief moment, capture the facial expression for the impression you're trying to create. You can work toward a goal of characterizing any individual as fitting into any image you want, whether it's smart, stupid, brash, reasonable, clumsy, deft, too old, too young, bigoted, impartial, sincere, hypocritical, caring or arrogant; whatever your goal is. And, believe me, that is what the news is doing every day with impunity and without conscience.

You can use talk shows, advertising, movies, sitcoms, or any show to highlight socialist thinking, molding the impression that people who think like that are accepted by the majority as intelligent, fair-minded, prudent, and popular, and view any other way of thinking as inspired by selfishness, racism, hatred, ignorance or some disability. Over a sufficient period of time, you can convince many people that this is just the modern way of thinking that the majority see as right and proper. That is very effective at discouraging resistance. You can label anyone with any connection to a field in which you're trying to further an agenda as an expert or scientist and you can describe the motive of anyone not in agreement as racist, xenophobic, or ignorant of science.

As the left-wing news media seeks to build socialism one step at a time, the next element will begin to arise, driven by a pressing need that no one had been concerned about. Suddenly, it becomes a matter of great public concern, with experts and scientists deeply bothered; a burgeoning problem that, if not dealt with, will be our undoing; a need backed by an alarming plethora of facts and figures.

Propaganda is powerful. Do you realize that most of the changes toward socialism were made in the face of the reluctance of the majority? Most didn't really want it but were conditioned to believe that the voice for them was so overwhelmingly powerful that it was useless to give any persistent resistance.

The politicians who enact our legislation are subject to the same influence of the media. Most of the major means of communicating news have fallen so much under liberal control that politicians are often afraid to say what they really feel because they know that they will get bad coverage. When the media exerts that kind of control at the helm, the main difference between a democratic and a republican administration is the speed at which we are advancing toward socialism.

What should concern us the most is the speed at which we are advancing toward atheism. The Bible plainly warns us that there is a spiritual war being waged. The church has to realize that if we don't make the truth of Christ heard, our culture will change and the people will be corrupted, and our enemy works fast. The devil always has some device working to divert people's attention away from worshipping God and the speed at which he works will leave you wondering in amazement, "What happened?"

Chapter 11

Expect Opposition

I'm writing the most about the socialist controlled media because it is the largest existing factor that we face in opposition to the revival of fundamentalist Christianity. It is certainly not the only thing in the arsenal of the enemy, but it is the largest strategically organized resistance we face at the present time. Everyone who wants to see revival needs to know where the most effective resistance will come from and what methods to be prepared for. Socialism is really no worse than many other things that have resisted Christ down through the centuries, but it certainly has gained a lot of ground in the space of one lifetime. It would be worth our time to look at the strategy they have used in the past to prepare us for what to expect in the future as they attempt to silence us.

The overall goal has always been the same: to prepare us for a worldwide socialist government by wearing down cultural, racial, and religious differences, indoctrinating us in socialist thought, and using every method possible to make us perceive the world as interdependent and becoming more secular and socialist as it matures toward unity.

At the time I was born, they still had not made much headway at changing the mindset of America. Most of the adults I knew as a small boy had lived through the Great Depression and I believe that most were convinced that some government intervention was needed as a stimulus to keep the private economy moving well. But they still considered this to be a free enterprise nation and only wanted government big enough to provide a healthy economic impetus and ensure fairness. They also overwhelmingly thought of us as a "Christian Nation." The expanded and more liberal government that we had at that time was not seen in any way to conflict with our conception of a Christian nation.

The United States, after the First World War, never joined the League of Nations, preferring to stay out of political involvement with the rest of the world, despite President Wilson's attempts to lead us into it, and calling the war, "the war to end all wars." But by the end of the Second World War, organized socialism was in a much stronger position. That war brought us into the age of atomic weapons, and we emerged as unquestionably the world's most powerful nation.

With the threat of nuclear annihilation, a real possibility in a world with communist dictatorships vowed and determined to take over and control the world, our participation in the United Nations was assured. The American people had come into a position where we felt like we had to be involved with the rest of the world as the peacekeeper and defender of democracy. It had finally become easy to make people feel that, as a nation of such international influence, we had a responsibility to bring the world together, working through secular political channels.

The attack on the Christian faith had not gained much ground and I'm sure that most people would probably not realize that it even existed. But by the time I was old enough to vote, the seeds that had been sowed were rapidly starting to germinate. Most of the largest newspapers were under liberal control, a lot of headway had been gained in education, and the first step in the attack on the faith was underway. Few people in the churches realized how busy the forces of socialism had been with an organized plan.

The attack began, not as an ostensible attack on Christianity, but rather an attack on "fundamentalism." If they could destroy the foundation, the belief that Jesus Christ and the Holy Spirit are real and the Bible is literally true, they could open the door to change the faith into secular socialism without ever changing the name.

They began a massive campaign to convince people that the Bible, rather than having been inspired by the Holy Spirit, was simply the product of men; sometimes weaving things that might have occurred into a fairy tale by expansion, sometimes as propaganda to fuel an agenda, and sometimes to give an explanation for things they didn't understand in more primitive times. In this modified appreciation of the Bible, God's existence is not denied, but our concept of inspiration is.

The plan was never to represent themselves as opponents who were trying to destroy the faith but rather as enlightened, well educated, and knowledgeable Christians within the faith. That the Bible is often erroneous was simply stated to be a fact known to science.

This strategy works on the same principle as a socialist effort to enact an unconstitutional law. The strategy is never to amend the constitution to allow it—which would expose the amendment to individual state votes—but rather to just keep calling it a constitutional right until people can be persuaded that, at least, a lot of other people think it is. Put into practice long enough this will change the unconscious perception of many that nothing is being changed, but rather growing in the way that it was always meant to.

To change the Christian outlook, they simply harp on the idea that the insistence on following God's word, if it conflicts with their agenda, is seen by most as harsh, judgmental, hypocritical, and counterproductive. If we really loved others, we would not let our loyalty to God's principles offend them because that would be seen as imposing our beliefs on them.

It is not presented so as to make one feel that we have to choose between faith and atheism. One can still believe that the Bible is "truth," but often not "the truth," often containing real human wisdom, but not always a reliable guide in a complex, changing world.

This leads to more and more distraction from the central spiritual message into such things as questioning whether the writers understood things known to modern science in describing Jesus's healing disease or casting out demons. It is most effective among those who have not really read the Bible enough to see the real meaning. If you harp on it long enough, they will develop a subliminal perception that the Bible is all about miracles that supposedly happened in the dim past that strain the imagination of reasonable minds. It is easy to convince such people that a fundamentalist is someone who will strain at a gnat and swallow a camel because he believes that man is not supposed to ever contemplate or think for himself in matters of morality.

The ultimate goal is to subvert us from the church of Jesus Christ to an agnostic, secular, socialist organization while still calling ourselves the Christian church. Eventually, we will become a group of people who no longer believe in divine inspiration or a God who is active in any way. Any interest in the Bible is from intellectual curiosity about the ethos that shaped our western culture before the modern era of science.

Back in the 1800s several types of Bible criticism were developed. They sought to examine Bible narratives by looking to see if there was any textural indication that an account could have been written at a different time than first thought or by a different author. This has been hyped into a science that is not, and they have now worked it into some of the main seminaries that preacher candidates have to attend to be ordained; and they, frankly, have succeeded in shutting the Holy Spirit out of some of the mainstream churches.

I remember reading, as an adolescent, a Sunday school lesson in the Methodist Church that stated that some of the New Testament epistles were not written by the ascribed author, but rather at a considerably later date, and that it was a common practice at the time to attach the name of a Bible character whom the author thought might have expressed what he was saying in a similar manner.

It really diminishes the weight of scripture when you read, for instance, that Peter's letter in which he gives an eyewitness account of the voice from heaven that he and those with him heard about Jesus, and you read that this was most likely written by someone two centuries later trying to emulate the manner of expression he thought the legendary Peter would have used. This plan has been faithfully followed to try to convince us that there are no real accounts of actual events in the Bible, only twists that were added after actual events to become folklore.

When I read that lesson, it was simply stated as something universally assumed by expert Bible scholars to be almost certainly true. I have since sometimes ran into other occasions when the author attempted to explain why experts doubt the authenticity of something and it has never really made sense to me when I tried to follow their reasoning that their theories should disprove the Bible.

The Book of Daniel is a good example of how non-believers, calling themselves scholars and experts, are destroying the work of the Holy Spirit. I went to a Bible study in the Methodist Church one time about Daniel. The study was taken from a book with a picture of the Roman god Janus on the cover, looking both ways, past and future.

We were told at the beginning that Daniel couldn't have been written at the time purported because some of the musical instruments mentioned in 3:5 were not known at that time. The instruments named were the horn, pipe, lyre, sackbut, psaltery, and the dulcimer. In another translation the first three are called the cornet, flute, and harp. I'm not sure whether anyone would know for sure what they all were, or how they would compare to the nearest modern version. Some Bible critic, however, figured out and extensively researched to prove his point, that this was the first mention of one or more of them that we could find, but there is no real reason to believe that they could not have been known at the time of Nebuchadnezzar.

We were told that Daniel was written in a style that was used at the time where they wrote of things of the past using the future tense as if it were predictions of the future (or something like that) to make a point. We were told that Daniel was written at the time of the Maccabean revolt, and from the explanation we got, we didn't know whether it was to encourage and rally support or to discourage. Nothing made any sense. About all we learned was that there was, supposedly, no knowledge of the book until that time and then it began to be rapidly circulated.

If you just read the book with an open mind and assume that it goes back to the time of the Chaldean Empire, it all makes sense. And if it were written at the time of the Maccabean revolt, around 167 B.C., ask yourself this; how did the writer know how long it would be from the time given in the book, a decree of Artaxerxes, given about 278 years prior, until the Messiah? I will say a little more about that in a later chapter.

Another objection that is sometimes used to discredit the book is that the king in Babylon after the overthrow of the Chaldeans was called Darius. Cyrus is generally accepted in history as the first Persian king. It seems obvious to me that Darius was appointed to be king in Babylon by Cyrus and, according to tradition, took a throne name. He was a Mede and Cyrus was a Persian. The two nations were allied at the time of the Babylonian conquest and Cyrus, who was chief military commander, continued to expand the empire in that capacity and was the Persian "King of Kings." Darius was probably Cyaxares II, a Mede, who was sixty-two years old at the time. Daniel in 5:31 says, "And Darius the Mede, received the kingdom, being about threescore and two years old." That indicates an appointment, not a conquest.

He was made king in Babylon when it fell with Belshazzar as co-regent. Nabonidus, who had resided in Arabia while Belshazzar, his son, reigned in Babylon, gave military resistance to Cyrus for a while after the fall of Babylon.

We have accounts from several Greek and other historians and sometimes differing versions of events are given. Some indicate that Cyrus first conquered the Medes and then Babylon, and others that the Medes and Persians were allies. The statuary in the palace at Persepolis indicates that they were allies and equals at the time. One Babylonian historian, who was probably closer to the situation than any of the others, said that when Nabonidus surrendered to Cyrus, he was given the kingdom of Carmania, but Darius, the king, took part of it for himself.

If you try to research Daniel on the internet, you will probably be told early on that most experts consider it to be fiction. When you have accounts of things in the Bible that are far enough removed, that particular details would be hard to prove, you will find that the naysayers are usually labeled as experts, scientists, and scholars.

If you can get enough of this worked into a church's Sunday school lessons and preachers convinced that parts of the Bible are not true, you can eventually take away all enthusiasm. You may have individual members left who believe, but the church, as an effective spreader of the gospel of Christ will be dead.

It all comes down to this; God, who was able to create a universe that works in an orderly fashion is able to see to it that the Bible contains what He wants it to say. If you read it, pray and meditate on it with an open mind, you will believe it!

While the attack to convince us of the unauthenticity of the Bible goes on, there is also a relentless campaign to create a bad image for fundamentalist believers. A fundamentalist is depicted as someone who, because of an ingrained chauvinist attitude, is held captive to his own stubborn insistence that something, obviously full of flaws to the scientific mind, must be adhered to without question; a person who refuses any reasonable examination of scientific evidence. He is portrayed as a prisoner of his own superstitions; one you can't reason with because of a paranoid fear of finding out that any part of his beliefs might not be right, and it is ingrained in his mind that anything that presents a challenge to them must be met with blind resistance or violence. That science and learning prove the fundamentalist wrong is always represented as a certain fact simply by stating it to be so, and picturing most of the world as agreeing.

Another line of attack is a never-ending campaign to make Christians feel that any attempt to spread the gospel or to preserve parts of our culture that reflect the Christian faith is intolerant, bigoted, and oppressive. The present strategy of socialism in America today is to try to bring as many diverse people as possible into our society. Their favorite word to describe this policy is "inclusive."

The ultimate goal is a guided homogenization. All these diverse groups are supposed to be drawn to abandon any adherence to their own creed in a society that has become too pluralistic and disunited to work and be drawn together into an atheist society with no moral concepts other than those projected by the socialist media. Anything seen as being resistant to this is characterized as an attack on the rights of others to have their own beliefs and force them into yours.

No society is going to hold together and function without a sense of commonality of conviction and purpose. God has told us from the time that Israel and the Mosaic law began that if people don't put God first and reverence the way He has shown us, it will fall apart. What socialism is trying to do is replace a society that acknowledges God and His laws with one that doesn't and will be held together with laws and customs that the enemy of God inspires.

The society that God outlines for us, if He is followed, builds and maintains moral character and responsibility in us as individuals and the society that His enemy inspires will eventually fall apart. The manipulators of the socialist propaganda machine want you to believe, and they do believe themselves, that socialism is the matrix of human wisdom that will finally evolve this world into utopia, but it isn't. All these things are going to play out just like God said. There is a reason Moses said to study this law and get the sense of it!

Another line of attack, and this may be the main one, will be to label any attempt at Christian revival as the product of "white racism." This is the universally favored tool of the socialist movement.

The initial founding concept of socialism was that society was unjust because of economic inequalities; that it was not fair to allow some to have more material worth simply because they had been more successful or had better opportunity. But in America there never has been enough economic class resentment for socialism to harness the kind of class struggle they need. Most of us are content with the free enterprise system.

It is much more effective to use race. That is because of one natural aspect of human nature, the fact that all people have an attachment and sense of belonging to a race, which they feel is an extension of the family. That is human nature and not, per se, unjust. Injustice is when you fail to do unto others as you would have them do unto you.

Socialist propaganda always tries to project the image that as long as a scintilla of that feeling of familial bond exists within you, you are a racist. The strategy is to persistently portray white people as racists, but black people only as victims of racism. It creates an enormous amount of frustration for both of them because both are racists to the same extent without meaning spite to each other.

The core of Christian morality and values is the acceptance of individual responsibility for the inner person that you are. In contrast, socialist propaganda creates imagery assigning responsibility to a group. The imagery of group hatred and destructive intentions they portray and manipulate as patent racism in America today is a handy tool to keep moving us toward a socialist agenda. White people are conditioned to soften any resistance for fear that it will be seen as blatant racial hatred and black people will not resist for fear that any chances they have for fair participation and advancement will be destroyed.

Socialist propaganda has always sought to control and manipulate African Americans to their advantage, and they will certainly try it to counter any perceived spiritual revival of Christianity. You can expect to see more imagery from the media labeling any spiritual revival as the product of white supremacists and far right extremists.

Another opposition to revival that we can expect will be from the "Gay Community." It may seem almost unbelievable to many of us that this development in our culture has come so far in such a short period of time, but it is not surprising when you follow the natural progression of the sexual revolution that began in the 1960s.

There is good reason for following and holding sacred God's guidelines for sexual conduct. Young people in America were lured into thinking that if they could get around the immediate responsibility that goes with bringing children into existence that there would be no serious consequences. But God made us so that it fills a deeply innate psychological need to live in earnest commitment to spouse, to family, and to Him in the bonds of marriage. When we start practicing our own experimentation, we destroy that.

When we start trying to live contrary to the way we know is acceptable to God we become uncomfortable with ourselves. We start slipping away from the church. We become more ambivalent about resisting things we know to be perverted when we don't feel right about what we are doing ourselves. We become ill at ease teaching children when we are not exemplary in our own living. Pretty soon the custom of parental responsibility to teach boys how to grow up to be what a man should be and girls to be what a woman should be, as well as every other aspect of Christian doctrine, is no longer passed along. The end-result is that socialism is teaching sexuality to children in school instead of parents at home.

Many of us never think of Christian doctrine as scientific but it is. The word "science" means knowledge and Christian science comes from the One who made us and understands better than anyone else how the human mind works, and what leads to fulfillment and peace of mind. That science tells us that as children begin to mature sexually, they are facing a new, unknown part of living, and need guidance and counseling. They need help to face this new part of maturing so they can know with assurance what is expected of them and what are the reasonable bounds of conduct.

What they are being taught in school is the physical nature of sexuality and that some people just have a natural inclination to be attracted sexually to their own gender.

If having sexual relations is going to be considered a right and marriage just a choice that is still available, with nothing sacred about it, why shouldn't people who have different ideas about what sex is have the same right? Next, it stands to reason that they should be able to marry. Then, if that is going to be considered a perfectly normal and acceptable part of our society, why shouldn't they be allowed to adopt children?

How many young persons today are facing the challenge of sexual maturing with no real help or encouragement to become a manly man or womanly woman? How many will decide that they may be homosexuals or lesbians because they are uncomfortable with the change to sexual maturity when this is the kind of guidance they get?

The lunacy that is working its way into some of our educational system is almost unbelievable. I just watched a news reel showing a man in one school explaining to a group in the lower grades that when you are born, the doctor makes a guess about your sex based on physical features, but that may turn out to be wrong later. Left unchallenged, this craziness that is being used to inculcate our children will completely take over. We are seeing more drawn into this web every day.

They will miss the personal sense of fulfillment and purposeful life that God intended and the self-perpetuating society that following Him nourishes will crumble and fall. Can you picture where America is headed with half of the adults living with their own sex and the rest as unmarried men and women living together and the few children they are having being indoctrinated in this way of thought?

The media has now become the spin doctor for this way of life. Cut on your T.V. and you will probably soon see a woman with a wife or female husband, a man with a husband or male wife, or people having sex change operations featured as the normal and perfectly acceptable way of life. It is portrayed as accepted in modern culture, based on both science and humane understanding of others. Any expression of opposition is condemned as arising from an unenlightened and hateful attitude. But it goes against Gods' word in the Bible and if we don't change course we will see the result of not heeding His word.

The church of Christ cannot be what He wants us to be if we just compromise and accept this as things you can do and also be a Christian. The media will use every available means to spin us as a radical sect, so consumed with our biases and hatred that we are a threat to freedom and democracy. They will also try to convey that the church is under the cultlike control of white male chauvinists and a threat to women's rights.

Leftist news agencies already censure the news by omission and representing as fact their reported opinion, but they are eying the possibility of gaining actual official censorship rights against expressing opinions. Anything not in alignment with their agenda is characterized daily in the news as inciteful, dangerous, insurrectionist, etc., and they are becoming increasingly vocal in their demands that it should be censured or outlawed.

If a great revival of Christian faith occurs in this country, we can expect to see all these tactics used in full force to destroy it. So how do we fight it?

Chapter 12

Rely on the Holy Spirit

The answer is, we don't. Jesus said to not resist evil. When we want to change something in the devil's world, he wants to lure us into a quarrel in which we respond using the words and tone of his world. Nothing will be accomplished but contention and ill will. The devil has those in his world prepared for automatic deafness to reason in spiritual matters. In 1 Corinthians 2:14 Paul wrote, "But the natural man receiveth not the things of the spirit of God; for they are foolishness to him, neither can he know them, for they are spiritually discerned."

The only way to change unspiritual people is to give them spiritual understanding, and only the spirit of God can do that. The Holy Spirit sees the minds of unspiritual men and knows when it is useless to speak.

In the eighth chapter of John, we have an account of Jesus teaching in the temple when a group of men brought a woman they said was taken in the act of adultery. They said that Moses said in the law that they should stone her and asked what He would say.

"This they said, testing Him, that they might have to accuse Him. But Jesus stooped down and with His finger wrote on the ground, as though He heard them not."

This woman was not brought in the spirit of obedience to the Mosaic law. The man with whom she was, was not brought in, and they were all aware that a person could be put to death only under Roman law at the time. At that time, they were all under Roman law by the will of God. The law given to Moses was plain that if they didn't obey the voice of the Lord, they would be put under the dominion of other nations. They wanted to force an issue of the Mosaic law to see if Jesus would prove to not be their idea of a messiah, and most likely just expected Him to back down so they could show that He wasn't.

This was purely a trap set for Jesus to trip Him up. So, He just said something that made them admit that without words, "He that is without sin among you, let him first cast a stone at her," and then he stooped down and wrote on the ground until they all had left.

They were not willing to stone her themselves and He refused to let them drag Him into an argument with no real purpose to heed God.

The church today has to realize in the same manner as Jesus in this account, that the devil is never interested in honest debate over how God thinks versus the way he has his world conditioned to think. We can't be dragged into this world if we're going to be the church of Christ. Jesus understood that it is useless to respond to what the devil stirs up and wrote in the sand. Nothing would have been accomplished if He had reacted any other way, and neither can we gain anything by responding to any challenge in a worldly way.

Look again at the lines of attack that I said we might expect in the last chapters. Who will you argue with to stop them? The attack on fundamentalism will continue full speed ahead, regardless of any attempts you might make to persuade them to be honest in their characterization. As sure as the world turns, they will continually try to conjure a mental association with intolerance, bigotry, rash behavior, and ignorance of science. None of this is done to challenge fundamentalists to prove themselves with response. It is simply the science of propaganda in its most effective form.

To try to argue with them about how they use race to fool us into socialism will not stop them. What they are doing works, and they will continue doing it. No amount of reasoning to explain what could be done that would work better and be fairer to all will change the course. It would be the very thing they would want you to say so they could twist it into wrong motive and a tacit admission of racism.

There is no one to argue with to explain why our traditional morals and customs regarding marriage and family life are better that will change their course. The way of life that is dragging us down every day will continue to be portrayed as the modern and acceptable way in the entertainment and news media, and we, as a nation, will continue being dragged into the mire.

Without the Holy Spirit, people will continue to give in to the carnal nature that influences us all. There are really very few people in the world who really don't have sense enough to see that the result of this way that we are now accepting will ruin us, but that won't stop it.

Children will continue to be taught in public institutions that the environment controls our fate, not personal responsibility and individual initiative, and that socialism is the environment needed. Textbooks in school will continue to present history that conveys the imagery of our American forebears, especially Christians, as unashamedly evil, racist, and greedy, whose actions must be atoned for by destroying the culture that made us great and replacing it with socialism.

The seminaries that do it now will continue to try to turn out preachers who are too intimidated to preach the real good news of Jesus Christ because they are led to believe that the Bible is not true. You'll still be seeing the same message aired in documentaries and worked into Sunday school lessons that "scholars" and "experts" know that the Bible is not true.

Socialist news agencies will continue to search high and low for happenings they can embellish and highlight to advance their agenda and ignore things that would detract. Some of the most incompetent commentators with histories of shady dealings will get good press because they go along with the overall agenda of the media while some of the best, most honest, will get nothing but constant detraction. The ones the media likes will be described as popular and the ones they don't like, even though they may be the most admired by the people, will be described as unpopular. The media will continue to twist the words of elected officials they don't like and create illusions of illegalities or treasonous dealings and pursue them relentlessly.

These things are causing many problems, and the solutions demanded will only make them worse, but our own efforts to change things without the Holy Spirit will only get us labeled busybodies who should mind our own business.

The Pharisees sought to gain God's favor by strict observance and enforcement of the law, but acted under their own zeal, not God's Spirit. There was a real belief among them that, if ever, just one Sabbath was properly kept, Messiah would then come, and they tried to make the people circumspectly comply in the very narrowest interpretation of the law.

The law was, of course, a good thing, but all the Pharisees ever accomplished was trying to beat a dead horse to death and all they achieved was ill will and division among the people. I believe they truly thought that they were serving God but, actually, they only played right into the devil's hands to keep both Israel, and the gentiles wrapped up in this world and away from God.

We are all like that. It is not hard to drag even Christians who have the Holy Spirit into contention over worldly things because we all reason and have opinions about the things that affect our daily living. It's a natural reaction that we all need to be aware of if we want to live by God's will.

Recently, I was at home by myself, and I cut the T.V. on. I decided to check out a channel that Katie sometimes watches, and I didn't know exactly where to find it, so I started using the automatic changer to find it. I stopped for a while and listened to a commentator on one of the liberal news channels, and in only a moment I had become absolutely furious.

When you hear someone say things that you consider to be a lie and malign the character of public figures that you agree with, the natural reaction is to get upset with the person who said it. My immediate reaction is that the man I'm hearing is lying and knows it, but in fact he really believes that presenting my views in a good and impartial light would lead us in a bad direction and his in a good one. He knows that he is not being impartial but really believes himself to be doing what is best. Such people really believe that if we can be brainwashed long enough by associating the motives of those not in agreement with socialist concepts as decadent and evil that the day will come when we will be led to unity and harmony with human wisdom and a changed perception of morality and will have no need of Christ.

Millions of others: politicians, schoolteachers, professors, butchers, bakers, and candlestick makers have been fooled and swayed from the truth by the same scheme. They are not like that simply because they love evil and hate good. They've just been misled by the one who wants our souls and hates Christ.

We are not in a struggle against opposing people. It's a struggle against spiritual forces. In the previous chapter I described how the devil has used socialism and other worldly developments to pull us away from following God. The devil knows that socialism will only eventually fail, ruin our economy, and destroy our moral fiber. He doesn't care whether you're a socialist or not. If socialism is defeated and its influence ends, he will corrupt us through whatever replaces it just as effectively. His objective is to keep you too distracted to see God and let His spirit in to set your priorities straight. This is a struggle about where your mind and spirit will be focused and who will control them. The devil is pretty good at misleading our focus.

Jesus said that the whole law hinged on two commandments, to love The Lord your God, and to love your neighbor as yourself, and I doubt that you would find a dedicated socialist in the world who would not consider himself to be in agreement with the second one. The struggle that Christians face is not against people. It is against the greatest con artist in the universe who gets his foot in the door by distracting us from the first commandment.

Almost every problem that is causing us a lot of trouble in today's society has arisen because we have set aside the first commandment and sought to go about practicing the second without it. When we do that, our carnal nature takes over and we are always led astray. Without God leading us in the way of spiritual wisdom and discernment, we will never do any better than we're doing now.

God knows how prone we are to be fooled and has provided the way for us to overcome, but it is up to us to use it. We face an enemy whose ability to deceive and corrupt is incredibly powerful. Don't think for a minute that you can take him on yourself. Acknowledge Christ and trust Him, and He will give you the Holy Spirit to dwell within you. That is the only way we will ever find the wisdom, guidance, and courage to change this nation.

When you look around and see how the devil has gained control of American culture and you ardently want to change it, ask yourself this; What would he want me to do?

I can tell you exactly what he wants you to do. He wants you to jump right in attacking those he has deceived, totally engrossed in how to fix America by destroying them instead of really turning us all to God. It doesn't really matter to him which side wins as long as we operate under our own power without the Holy Spirit.

America's problems can't be fixed without a spiritual revival. Jesus is not looking for a new and improved secular world. His purpose is to get you ready to be like the resurrected Christ, and if we will be asking and trusting Him to do that, the present world will be better also. The church used to understand that we are in spiritual warfare and have a duty to act for the Lord, both corporately and personally. An effective corporate church is simply one where the individual members are willing to be active participants led by the spirit and not part of this world. The goal of each Christian must be to first wholly commit to Christ, and next, to help build a church of committed people. Always be willing to lift Him up with thanksgiving and praise and belong to a church that lifts Him up. If a church is not there to reciprocate what He has done for us, praise and thank Him, and draw us to Him in a deeply personal way, it is of no use to Him or you. Make the church what it is called to be, and God will use it.

Understand the tactics the devil uses in the spiritual war. He speaks when he is in control and doesn't waste time arguing against the rightness of God's precepts and rules. It is a psychological war against the Holy Spirit, a propaganda war. His objective is to first divert your attention away from God onto his world. Then he wants to change your surroundings to keep your mind off of God, so you won't allow yourself to hear or consider God's voice.

His powers of deception are too strong for us without God's spirit. Remember that we are not fighting other people, we are fighting him, and he never identifies himself as the leader of those he fools, as Christ identifies with us. If you are not satisfied with the new surroundings he puts you in, He wants you to think that you are fighting socialists, the media, or whoever he is using and stir you to hatred for them. If we are not careful he will have us doing only that.

A major theme of this book is trying to build a more unified church that will use every practical outlet in America to spread the gospel. But that can be easily infiltrated by the enemy of Christ to lure us into his world if we are not wholly dedicated to follow the Holy Spirit. Remember that the devil controls the spirit of his world, and it is useless for us to fight him in his world on our own. Again, the only way to change people in a secular world and give them spiritual understanding is through the Holy Spirit.

The devil is now relentlessly doing all in his power to change our perception of morality and sin by taking our attention away from God and the Holy Spirit. When he can make us forget God he uses the natural lustful desires of the carnal nature to lead us to rely on a new illusion of right and wrong he creates that offers no challenge to our carnal nature. To accomplish this he wants to erase everything in our surroundings that keep us reminded of God and the wisdom of His word.

A preacher I know got a private school started in his church. He soon found that there are many parents wanting to enroll children in private school because they believe public schools are doing the children more harm than good. But he also found that many of the children had no exposure to the Christian lifestyle or concepts of right and wrong. That is where Satan is doing the most damage in America.

If you will read the book of Deuteronomy, which seriously warns of what God expects of His people, and earnestly consider what you are reading, you will see that the devil carries on a spiritual war, and we can win only if we stay focused on God. We must also see to it that our cultural surroundings keep us focused on Him. When the devil can get our minds off Him he can easily mislead and destroy us.

One of the most important things the church can do now is to realize that we have let that slip. We have to act like a people who believe in Christ. Help to make your church into one where people are won to Christ and enthusiastic by being so yourself. Try to generate interest and open discussion about our faith among peers. Try to make the things that show public acknowledgement of God evident again; prayer, asking the blessing at meals, teaching children, and trying to live your daily life by example. Young children need to hear parents speak of God in a manner that acknowledges Him as real and having authority over our daily living. We will never see America's recovery from cultural decline until we begin to see things like these become evident in our daily living again.

Have you ever thought about how much more the church's message centered on the wisdom of God and the result of following Him or Satan when the church was stronger? The old church made it much plainer that we are in a spiritual war and our enemy is Satan, who misleads those who oppose us. God's work with us in this world is to prepare us for the coming world and the church, when challenged, cannot afford to get sidetracked from this by Satan's distracting tactics. Don't waste time resisting evil the way the devil wants you to. Instead, let the Holy Spirit speak His wisdom through the church and write in the sand when the devil speaks.

Chapter 13

Motivation and Unity

I f a nation was under attack from an enemy and the military strategy the leadership followed was only losing ground, that strategy and leadership would be replaced by a new leadership that watched the tactics of the enemy and employed a forceful counter. Every Christian knows who the enemy is, and we can see clearly that he has his forces persistently following a well-organized and coordinated plan. But we are not countering his moves anywhere near the scale of the enemy. We're running behind on all fronts.

In the first place, we don't act in unity. We are called to, but we don't. Again, remember the words of Peter, "But ye are a chosen generation, a royal priesthood, an holy nation, a people of His own, that ye should show forth the praises of Him who hath called you out of darkness into His marvelous light." (1 Peter 2:9) That implies a basic unity of purpose.

Jesus considers His people who believe in Him "the church," and we all have a duty to try to unify and increase His kingdom. In Revelation when Jesus addresses the seven churches, I believe with all of my heart that it was directed at the church down through the era.

The Philadelphian church, He commended for their strength and faithfulness. This was a church on fire for Christ and working hard to follow Him, to keep alive the devotion to Him, and to increase. This was done in the face of the same factors that had caused others to retrogress, and it was because they had commitment and zeal.

The church from the reformation on was, in one way, becoming disunified. Christians had become divided into many denominations. Methodists, Baptists, Presbyterians, Moravians, and so many other churches had varying opinions of how some points of doctrine ought to be interpreted. But they were all united in that they believed that there was a spiritual warfare going on and they were all zealous for the cause of Christ.

Two things are saliently different now. The church has become lukewarm, less divided over points of doctrinal interpretation; and also, it has become far less unified in opposing worldly opposition. On the other hand, the enemy of Christ has gotten his forces more unified, carrying on the war through every available means, and shows himself to be dedicated, determined, and with well-directed coordination.

The enemy has gained an overwhelming amount of control: in education from kindergarten through college, in entertainment, news, the internet; his powerful influence is changing our culture, our perception of moral standards, our government and it is seen everywhere, all day and night, seven days a week. And much of the church is offering a whittled down gospel in a twenty-minute sermon once a week, trying hard not to offend anyone who might not agree, and doing no evangelizing. That is no way to counter!

Does anyone really think that our Lord is pleased with this kind of response to an enemy who has corrupted much of the nation to the likeness of Sodom and Gomorrah?

We're acting like we have no right to say anything that anyone might not want to hear, or to use anything other than our little Sunday get together to present the case for the gospel of Christ. The church today needs to wake up to our responsibility to use every means available to us to work for Christ. Our enemy certainly uses everything he can do to further his plans.

Have you ever thought about how much different our world might look today if Christ's people had been as intent and as thorough as the socialist movement has been at trying to indoctrinate by every means? What if people all around us clearly believed that God made us and were motivated to put the two commandments that Jesus said were most important first and in right order. With everyone believing in a God who, having made us to be like Him in a spiritual body, and knows our every thought, how much more sincere would we be with Him and each other in this carnal state? How much more value would we put in our own personal responsibility and our indebtedness to Him because of what Jesus has done for us?

How much sounder would the mental and spiritual health of our world be if children, as they grow to maturity, saw all around them unbroken families with parents taking responsibility to teach Christian principles to them. What if they were all being thoroughly taught the Christian responsibility of sexual morality, and the importance of being sure of devotion and commitment, both their own and of their spouse, before entering onto a sexual relationship in marriage?

What if children were not exposed in school, and through every other outlet that can be used to shove it in their faces, that homosexuality, lesbianism, bisexuality, being transgender, or whatever term you want to use, are perfectly normal and acceptable things? What if they were not encouraged to think about whether maybe they might have such leanings? What if the media didn't commend their courage to "be themselves" if they choose those things and strongly condemn the attitude of anyone who holds on to the Christian concept of sexuality?

What if, instead of "social studies," history was taught again, with no bias or characterization toward groups, but simply an accurate account of what happened? And what if students formed opinions from being taught the Christian concept of individual responsibility, as to what political or social agendas to support when they look at the past.

What if all political news that you read or watched on television or the internet tried to show as accurately as possible what the various political figures said, to give you a good understanding of all viewpoints, instead of the slanted propaganda that we get now? What if, instead of ignoring news that's damaging and exposes corruption for one side, or labeling it "disinformation," while treating a manufactured innuendo about the other side as serious news and a threat to our national security, whatever was said was just reported as having been said, and what was proved was reported as news? And what if there were no effort to deter looking for proof on one side and claiming that is already proved for the side they want you to believe?

What if when you watched your favorite programs on television you saw things that reflect more Christian family values? What if our churches were filled on Sunday and families were attending Sunday schools, and preachers and teachers everywhere were delivering Holy Spirit inspired sermons and teaching?

And what if every day sincere prayers were going up throughout the land in the name of Jesus?

It could be a lot more like that in America today! But it is going to take a new Woke movement; that is a church that has finally woke up to realize that we have to get involved in the spiritual war that Satan is waging and get in it to prevail, or we will wind up being outlawed and silenced as some sort of radical hate group.

Jesus did not die to save just the handful in America today who have heard and understood the gospel. We can't continue to not get the message out just because Satan wants us to think that no one wants to hear it, and we would be violating their rights if we try to tell them. Most of America today is headed straight to hell and we are the only ones who have anything to say that is sensible and true. We owe it to them to try our best to get the message of Christ across. And believe it or not, we have as much right to try to influence the way people think and to try to change our culture according to our view as the liberal media.

Now I want to stress again an important point in this book. Compromise with the world and its false teachings have brought many churches in America today to the lukewarm state that Jesus says He will spew out. But there are still many true Christians and there are still many church leaders and preachers who haven't been deceived and would like to see a real Holy Spirit led revival in America. The Holy Spirit has not deserted His people, and the church is not dead yet.

I believe that our Lord wants some of our best positioned church leaders to begin a unified and organized effort to strengthen the fundamentalist Christian outreach, and, like organized socialism, to expand our influence using every prudent means we can, both inside and outside the church walls. The cultural changes pulling us to secularism were not achieved by overt debate with the church to convince people their way was better. They were achieved using the things of the world to lure us away from God. Spiritual understanding and wisdom are what draws us to God, but we should also use worldly things, when it is spiritually wise, to draw people to them.

God has put us all in this world and expects us to work for Him within its confines. In chapter 16 of Luke, after the parable of the steward who was accused of mismanagement by his employer, Jesus said,

> And I say unto you, make to yourselves friends by the mammon of unrighteousness, that when it fails, they may receive you into the everlasting habitations. He that is faithful in that which is least is faithful also in much; and he that is unjust in the least is unjust also in much.
>
> If, therefore, ye have not been faithful in the in the unrighteous mammon, who will

commit to your trust the true riches? And if ye have not been faithful in that which is another man's, who shall give you that which is your own?

No servant can serve two masters; for either he will hate the one and love the other, or else he will hold to the one and despise the other. Ye cannot serve God and Mammon. (Luke 16:9–13)

Look at how many worldly resources the enemy of Christ is using daily to deceive us and keep us away from God. Someone has to write the texts that many children have to see at an early age to sway them to sexual perversion. Someone has to write the social studies texts that condition them to think socialism is the path to world unity and harmony, and Christianity is not. Institutions have to be conditioned to prepare teachers to teach these things. The infiltration of colleges with Marxist leaning professors requires orchestration. Likewise, the infiltration of seminaries with teachers of false doctrine who use higher criticism to create doubt of the reliability of Scripture. News agencies have to be established or infiltrated with anchors, panelists, and writers to spread socialist propaganda and the overall program has to be carried out with coordination. Various groups have to be formed and given names that can be cited as scientists or experts to give credence to the urgent need for the socialist agenda. They have to gain enough influence in the advertising and entertainment industry to condition us to accept that the socialist viewpoint is the dominant theme that is shaping our culture today. Getting Woke advocates appointed to positions of influence in corporations and government requires coordinated effort.

When you consider the vastness of such an army with its multifarious workings and how it seems to work with such organized precision it is amazing. Moreover, I'm sure that all of the prominent operatives are well aware of the centralized direction of strategy. But is there so much as one who is aware that they are under the control of anything but their own human cleverness?

The point I'm making here is not that the church needs to do the same thing the enemy has done by wresting control of every institution of influence or establishing our own to compete with those of the world. The point is for us to make sure that when we try to compete, we do it under the direction of the Holy Spirit. Just as most of those persons working in the liberal propaganda machine think they are following their own plan, and can't see that they are destroying us, so will the spiritual enemy infiltrate and corrupt our efforts in the same way if we are not following the Holy Spirit. We can use any outlet He leads us to but must always be on guard that we are delivering His message, which is always clear, simple spiritual truth that leads to repentance and acceptance of Christ. The devil will want us to believe we can accomplish more by attuning the church to work more in sync with the world so he can get into it.

The main purpose of a more centralized and unified effort is because we are all supposed to be "the church." This is the way it was in the beginning, as recorded in the Acts of the Apostles. They were all acting together as one body under the direction of the Holy Spirit. They went where they were sent and said what the Spirit gave them to say. They knew they were going into hostile territory.

We must realize that we are the only ones who can really change what is wrong with America today. Just staying comfortably inside our own little churches and hoping to see it voted out is a great delusion. No political organization or movement is going to fix what is really wrong. We have to get motivated and united, start working for Jesus in the way the church was meant to, and bring the gospel of Christ to the nation again.

Chapter 14

What Kind of Revival Do We Need?

We can find a lot of insight into what the church needs to do to change the world today by looking at the last great revival. It began by the work of men like John Wesley, the man we usually credit with being the founder of the Methodist Church. John Wesley was certainly a religious man. He was a priest in the Church of England. He was a man who earnestly sought to live up to righteous standards, but he relied too much on self-will and, I believe, may have always had a lingering feeling that something was not quite right. He had never been a huge success as an evangelist.

He once accepted an assignment to minister to the colonists and American Indians in Georgia, and on the voyage over, he became impressed with a group of Moravians. In a frightful storm, when it looked like they were in serious danger of being capsized, he and the ship's crew were all visibly terrified, but the Moravians showed nothing but complete faith in Christ, praying and praising God in word and song. They had complete faith in Christ and trusted Him, whether they lived or died. It didn't change John Wesley immediately, but it made a lasting impression on him that was brought to fruition later.

His mission to America was mostly unsuccessful, and he found himself at odds with the church leadership there. When he returned to England, he remained an Anglican priest and his approach to religion stayed the same as before. He sought to gain the spiritual things he needed by stern self-discipline and ritualistic study of Scripture and prayer.

Everything changed for John Wesley one evening when he attended a Moravian service. He described his experience of May 24, 1738, in his diary,

> In the evening, I went, very unwillingly, to a Society on Aldersgate Street, where one was reading Luther's preface to the Epistle to the Romans. About a quarter before nine, while he was describing the change which God works in the heart through faith in Christ, I felt my heart strangely warmed. I felt I did trust in Christ, Christ alone, for salvation, and an assurance was given me that He had taken away my sins, even mine, and saved me from the law of sin and death.

It was as simple as that. After years of seeking righteousness that would please God, he finally realized that trusting in Christ was the only way to come to God. The only work that he needed was done when Jesus in final agony on the cross said, "It is finished!" There was nothing that he could do himself but to trust in Christ and surrender his life to Him.

When he did this, he began to see the Holy Spirit work. John Wesley's experience started one of the greatest revivals in history. In his church, the leadership was too focused on self-discipline and ritualism to reach the masses of people who didn't have time for that because they had to work so hard to support themselves.

When a new movement began that shifted to reliance on Christ's work and the power of the Holy Spirit, they began preaching the true gospel of full trust in Christ and it started a new, spiritually resurrected church that made a real difference in the world. The word *gospel* means good news, and when it was brought to a weary world through the work of the Holy Spirit, it was received with joy. Many churches have strayed from that.

The same thing can happen today but, as in Wesley's day, revival has to overcome the obstacles of the time. Two things, especially, are holding back the work of the Holy Spirit now that are different from then.

The first thing is the abundance of material things to distract us. In Wesley's day, the average person had only a tiny fraction of the things that nearly everyone has and takes for granted now. They had to work long hours every day. They didn't have automobiles, phones, electric lights, central air, vacuum cleaners, washers, dryers, wash and wear clothes, computers, television, movies, and myriads of little conveniences that are commonplace now. They warmed their houses and cooked with the wood they chopped. They ate food that required a lot more preparation than a lot we have now. They drank, washed, and bathed with water they pumped or drew from a well. They traveled with horses they had to feed. Men, women, and children all had to work much harder with almost no leisure time, compared to our world now. We just simply live in a world that has immeasurably more competition to divert our attention away from our need for the church and Christ than they did then.

The other thing holding back the work of the spirit is our abundance of instant communication. There is more "information" available to the average person now in a day or so than people used to get in a year; far more than anyone really has time to absorb. It has to be something that really upsets us before we even bother to contend with anything we hear or read. We just accept it as something we can no more stop than birds singing or raindrops falling. It's just part of everyday life now.

That is why we have become the lukewarm church. We are so inured with hearing that "science" has now disproved a lot of the essential beliefs of the Christian faith that we don't resist it. We've seen and heard so much propaganda to convince us that everyone else now has a different concept of morality that we've started believing it. The truth is that there are still many whose concept hasn't changed but they are not making any effective protest because they've been conditioned to think that what they're hearing represents the self-determined, unalterable course of the majority, who are only exercising their rights; that it is improper and offensive to resist their influence on society in any way publicly, and that the only right Christians have is to practice their own beliefs in church, not in any way that might clash with the world.

The people the media represent as the majority are not really convinced of anything. They've just simply lost touch with the truth because it looks like life is easy and agreeable without it and burdensome with it. They've been too distracted by the world to listen to the voice of God and once that happens it's easier to stay hidden than to face the truth.

It's amazing how far we will let this carry us. That is why I am suggesting that fundamentalist church leaders try to unite in an organized front. We need to seek the will of God to be sure we are using every means within His will to reach this nation with the gospel of Jesus Christ, both within and outside the walls of the church.

Every social or political "ism" has to attain a prevalent portion of society in agreement; ideally all; and they must attain a culture that conforms to their beliefs. The devil knows that and is actively working to erode us away. The church seems to have forgotten it. We can't continue to exist as a tiny, unobtrusive segment of society that is viewed as out of touch in our way of thinking. We have to wake up and realize that if we care about this nation, we can't just let what's happening continue. Somehow, we've got to get the gospel of Christ heard again.

Too many of our mainstream churches in America today have come under the delusion that they can keep people from slipping away using the voice of the world in a spirit of compromise, but what does our Lord say?

"So then, because thou art lukewarm, neither cold nor hot, I will spew thee out of my mouth. Because thou sayest, I am rich and increased with goods, and have need

of nothing, and knowest not that thou art
wretched, and miserable, and poor, and
blind, and naked, I counsel thee to buy of
me gold tried in the fire, that thou mayest be
rich; and white raiment, that thou mayest be
clothed, and that the shame of thy nakedness
do not appear; and anoint thine eyes with
salve, that thou mayest see. As many as I love,
I rebuke and chasten; be zealous, therefore,
and repent. (Rev. 3:16-19)

The Holy Spirit is the only one who will bring us to real
restoration. He is the only one who can speak effectively
through us the word that will change the heart. Without
Him we will only lead astray and be led astray ourselves.

The leadership of some of our churches in America
today would do well to consider some of the words of Paul,
who founded churches in an environment even worse than
ours. Paul understood who called him and what his calling
was. It is the only calling that God gives, and that is to be
used by the Holy Spirit.

In First Corinthians 2:4–5 he says, "And my speech and
my preaching was not with enticing words of man's wisdom,
but in demonstration of the spirit and of power, that your
faith should not stand in the wisdom of men, but in the
power of God."

There are far more people in the world today who are
thirsting to hear that than there were in the days of John
Wesley and far more ways to reach them than in the days
of the circuit riders in America. If the church today will
pursue a new revival under the direction of the Holy Spirit

with the same dedication, far more people can be brought to Christ.

The devil knows how to make it look like the whole country has gone wholesale solidly to his side and there is no use in us trying to change anything, but just as in John Wesley's day, there are millions of miserable souls who need Jesus, and if we will come to Him in unity and faith asking, God will show us how to take the Holy Spirit to them. We must restore what's missing most in today's churches, the lordship of Jesus, the deep personal love for Him, and trusting our whole lives to Him.

Chapter 15

Prophecy

At a time such as this, when the devil seems to be winning and the church appears to be in danger of collapse, a lot of people find themselves becoming preoccupied with prophecy of the future in the Bible. The Bible is plain in telling us that in the last days there will be a falling away and an apostate church. But prophecy should be read to inspire another revival of the Christian church by opening you up to the Holy Spirit, not scaring you into looking for your own defensive measures.

All Bible predictive prophecy is already fulfilled except the events at the very end. As Moses prophesied, the Jewish people were scattered, and now the nation of Israel has begun again. The succession of world empires that Daniel prophesied has been fulfilled. We're seeing the apostacy of the church. When I was a boy in school these things were all true, but the setting of the stage described by prophesy was not quite complete. Now it is, but there is no defense. Living and working for Jesus is all we can do.

In the early days of the church at Thessalonica, they had become preoccupied with an idea that had gotten started that the day of the Lord was to be right away, and it was taking their minds off the most important things.

In the second chapter of Second Thessalonians Paul said,

"Now we beseech you brethren, by the coming of our Lord Jesus Christ, and by our gathering together unto Him, that ye be not soon shaken in mind, or be troubled, neither by spirit, nor by word, nor by letter as from us, as that day of the Lord is present. Let no man deceive you by any means, for that day shall not come, except there come the falling away first, and that man of sin be revealed, the son of perdition. Who opposeth and exalteth himself above all that is called God, or that is worshipped, so that He, as God, sitteth in the temple of God, showing Himself that He is God. Remember ye not that, when I was yet with you, I told you these things? And now ye know what restraineth that He may be revealed in His time. For the mystery of iniquity doth already work; only he who now hindereth will continue to hinder until he be taken out of the way. And then shall that wicked one be revealed, whom The Lord shall consume with the spirit of His mouth and shall destroy with the brightness of His coming. Even Him whose coming is after the work of Satan with all power and

signs and wonders, and with all deceivable-
ness of unrighteousness in them that perish,
because they received not the love of the
truth, that they might be saved.

For this cause, will God send them strong
delusion, that they should believe the lie.
That they might be judged who believed not
the truth but had pleasure in unrighteousness." (2 Thess. 2:1-9)

Paul then thanks God for calling them, giving them the
gospel of His word, and exhorts them to stand and hold
fast the traditions they had been taught. The paramount
thing, then as now, was to always be living for Christ, as if
He were coming right away.

When Paul refers to what restrains as "He who restraineth
and will continue to until He is taken out of the way," he
is referring to the Holy Spirit. In the first letter to the
Thessalonians, 4:13 through 18, Paul says,

"But I would not have you to be ignorant,
brethren, concerning those who are asleep,
that ye sorrow not, even as others who have
no hope, for if we believe that Jesus died and
rose again, even so them who also sleep in
Jesus will God bring with Him.

For this we say unto you by the word of
the Lord, that we who are alive and remain
unto the coming of the Lord shall not pre-
cede them who are asleep. For the Lord
Himself shall descend from heaven with a

shout, and the voice of the archangel, and with the trump of God; then we who are alive and remain shall be caught up together with them in the clouds, to meet the Lord in the air; and so, shall we be ever with the Lord."

Before the great tribulation, which Jesus affirmed will come in the last 7 years, the faithful believers will be taken out of the world, and God's Holy Spirit, which restrained, will be taken away with them. Paul counsels that it is useless for them to try to know the time or season because that day would come as a thief in the night, at a time when they are saying peace and safety, and sudden destruction will come upon them like labor pains, and there will be no escape.

Predictive prophecy is never given for us to know when or how to prepare for an event. Always remember that our enemy is good at fooling people and even the most dedicated Christians can't see through all the deceptions he brings, and the end will come when the world is saying peace and safety. Jesus said that, if it were possible, even the very elect would be deceived.

A prophecy of this time is found in the ninth chapter of Daniel. Daniel had been praying a long prayer of confession for himself and for his people, the Jews, who were then living in exile, and asking God to restore them. The angel Gabriel then appeared to him, because he was "greatly beloved," with the revelation that seventy weeks were determined on his people.

"Seventy weeks are determined upon thy people, and upon thy Holy City, to finish the transgression, and to make an end of sins, and to make reconciliation for iniquity, and to bring in everlasting righteousness, and to seal up the vision and prophecy, and to anoint the most holy.

Know, therefore, and understand, that from the going forth of the commandment to restore and rebuild Jerusalem to messiah, the prince, will be seven weeks and threescore and two weeks; the street shall be built again in troublous times.

And after threescore and two weeks shall Messiah be cut off, but not for himself; and the people of the prince that shall come shall destroy the city and the sanctuary, and the end of it shall be with a flood, and unto the end of the war, desolations are determined.

And he shall confirm the covenant with many for one week; and in the midst of the week, he shall cause the sacrifice and the oblations to cease, and for the overspreading of abominations he shall make it desolate, even until the consummation, and that determined shall be poured out upon the desolate" (Daniel 9:24-27).

We are not told that this was going to be exact timing that could be checked with a stopwatch, but from what we can see the events are told with eerie closeness and may be right to the very day for all we know. We are not really sure of exact dates that far back. Most events have to be timed by such statements as a numbered year in the reign of a monarch. Most scholars now think we are a little off in our calendar that is supposed to be based on the year of Christ's birth. A week is 7 periods of 360 days. Rev. 11:2-3 describes the last half week as 42 months, or 1260 days. Thus, a week is 360 times 7, or 2520 days. The time given for the commandment of Artaxerxes allowing the rebuilding of Jerusalem is usually considered to be 445 B.C., about 94 years after the prophecy was given.

From then to Messiah, which means anointed one, will be 483 years. If you take 445 and add 30 years to the time in A.D. when Jesus was baptized, or anointed, by John and the spirit was seen descending on Him and convert that to years of 360 days, you will be very close to 69 weeks of years.

After that, Messiah was cut off with nothing for himself (the crucifixion). Jerusalem was destroyed by the Roman legions about 70 A.D. (the people of the prince that shall come), and unto the end of the war, desolations are determined. The last seven years determined on the Jewish people occur at the end of the age and culminate with the second coming of Christ.

At the end of Daniel another, longer prophecy ends with the things that occur in the midst of the last week. Jesus affirmed this time of tribulation in Matthew 24. The church will be raptured before that.

The purpose of prophecy is not to show you in advance what's going to happen in the world, and it's not to tell you when the end of this age will be, so you'll know when to shape up. No one will be able to recognize for sure when those things start. It's simply to let you know that God is ultimately in control of all things.

Prophecy is not just predictive of future events. Anything the Holy Spirit inspires is prophecy. The whole Bible, with its history, psalms of praise, outlines of belief and conduct for the church, and predictions is prophecy. When a spirit led preacher or teacher has prayed and opens himself to the Holy Spirit, that is prophecy. Predictive prophecy is there to help strengthen your faith so you can take heed of all the Holy Spirit says and does for your guidance.

Look at David's Psalms. In the Psalm 22 we have a poignant picture of how Jesus felt in agony on the cross. You can see the priest who wagged his head and mocked because God was not delivering Him. Nailed and tied to the tree with all of His bones pulled out of joint, His dried tongue sticking to His jaws, His heart seeming to melt like water, and the soldiers casting lots for His garments. With every fiber in His body in intense pain, He gasped for breath until He no longer had the strength.

In Psalm 69, we see Him resurrected and delivered from the horrible pit with a new song in His heart. Then it reflects again on His anguish on the cross; hated and despised, as He became our sins, to be crucified; a stranger to His brethren and an alien to His mother's children. The ninth verse brings to mind when He overturned the tables of the moneychangers in the temple in sudden anger because He wanted so much their worship to be what it should. When that happened this verse came vividly to the minds of the disciples, "For the zeal of thine house has eaten me up; and the reproaches of those who reproached thee are fallen upon me." (Psalms 69:9, John 3;17)

Jesus went willingly to Jerusalem, knowing that the events that would unfold would lead to his cruel treatment and death on the cross. He did it so that we could be forgiven and live forever, free from the curse of sin that keeps us from blessing.

We would all do well to consider that He did it fully human, as one of us; consider Psalm 69 verses 16 through 28.

"Hear me, O Lord, for thy lovingkindness is good. Turn unto me according to the multitude of thy tender mercies.

And hide not thy face from thy servant; for I am in trouble. Hear me speedily. Draw near unto my soul and redeem it; deliver me because of mine enemies.

Thou hast known my reproach, and my shame, and my dishonor; Mine adversaries are all before thee.

Reproach hath broken my heart, and I am full of heaviness; and I looked for some to take pity, but there was none; and for comforters, but I found none.

They gave me also gall for my food, and in my thirst, they gave me vinegar to drink.

Let their table become a snare before them; and that which should have been for their welfare, let it become a trap.

Let their eyes be darkened, that they see not; and make their loins continually to shake.

Pour out thine indignation upon them, and let thy wrathful anger overtake them.

Let their habitation be desolate and let none dwell in their tents.

For they persecute him whom thou hast smitten, and they talk to the grief of those whom thou hast wounded.

Add iniquity unto their iniquity and let them not come into thy righteousness.

Let them be blotted out of the book of the living, and not be written with the righteous"

Let these words always cause us to remember that the willing sacrifice and death that Jesus endured for us was done while He subjected Himself to be and feel exactly as we. He would not have done it if it were not the only way to bring us face-to-face with our need to repent in earnest and turn our lives over to the only one who can save us. It was no easier for Him than it would be for you.

If this is not enough, don't we deserve not to come into His righteousness and be blotted out of the book of the living? And even when we respond the way He accepts, we are still not saved by our own righteousness.

Hebrews says,

For if we sin willfully after we have received the knowledge of the truth, there remaineth no more sacrifice for sins, but a certain fearful looking for judgement and fiery indignation, which shall devour the adversaries.

He that despised Moses' law died without mercy under two or three witnesses; Of how much sorer punishment, suppose ye, shall he be thought worthy, who hath trodden under-foot the Son of God, and hath counted the blood of the covenant, with which he was sanctified, an unholy thing, and hath done despite unto the spirit of grace? (Hebrews 10:26–29)

The entire Bible is prophecy, and its purpose is to lead us all to that question. God made us and He made us so that we could be with Him as His beloved children. He has provided the way, and we must choose Him of our own free will.

This is a very personal thing. In this day when we are all used to hearing some knowledgeable expert expound in a documentary why a gospel writer said what he did with his own slant because he was trying to cultivate the mindset of a particular group it's easy to lose touch with that. But the Bible means what it says, and it speaks to us all in a very personal way. God wants you to come to Jesus in that kind of relationship. Don't overanalyze it, just hear what the Holy Spirit is saying to you.

Jeramiah 31:31–33 says,

> Behold, the days come, saith The Lord, that I will make a new covenant with the house of Israel, and with the house of Judah, Not according to the covenant that I made with their fathers in the day that I took them by the hand to bring them out of the land of Egypt, which, my covenant, they broke, although I was an husband unto them, saith the Lord; But this is the covenant that I will make with the house of Israel; After those days, saith the Lord, I will put my law in their inward parts,

and write it in their hearts, and will be their God, and they shall be my people.

All prophecy is about the completion of God's work in us through the indwelling of His Holy Spirit. Paul says in the eighth chapter of Romans,

> For I reckon that the sufferings of this present time are not worthy to be compared to the glory which shall be revealed in us. For the earnest expectation of the creation waiteth for the manifestation of the sons of God.
>
> For the creation was made subject to vanity, not willingly but by reason of him who hath subjected the same in hope. Because the creation itself shall be delivered from the bondage of corruption into the glorious liberty of the children of God. For we know that the whole creation groaneth and travaileth in pain together until now.
>
> And not only they, but we ourselves also, who have the first fruits of the spirit, even we ourselves groan within ourselves, waiting for the adoption, that is, the redemption of our body. For we are saved by hope. But hope that is seen is not hope; for what a man seeth, why doth he yet hope for? But if we hope for that which we see not, then do we with patience wait for it.

Likewise, the Spirit also helpeth our infirmity; for we know not what we should pray for as we ought. But the Spirit himself maketh intercession for us with groaning which cannot be uttered. And he searcheth the hearts knowing what is the mind of the Spirit, because he maketh intercession for the saints according to the will of God.

And we know that all things work together for the good of them that love God, to them who are the called according to his purpose. For whom he did foreknow, he also did predestinate to be conformed to the image of his son, that he might be the first born among many brethren.

Moreover, whom he did predestinate, them he also called; and whom he called he also justified; and whom he justified, them he also glorified.

What shall we say then to these things? If God be for us who can be against us?

(Romans 8: 18-31)

What Paul is saying in these verses gives us the best understanding of what Bible prophecy is. That is the working of God's Holy Spirit to accomplish His final purpose for us.

When God made this creation, He subjected it to vanity. We were all made to live out a life in the physical body that we all have now. But our bodies and everything in this present world are going to die.

You may become a billionaire or the most powerful person in the world but one second after you die that is all gone. God has complete control of your fate then and you have nothing but the inner person you have become. In this present world God allows the devil to tempt us but he really has nothing to offer but a short-lived vanity here and everlasting misery afterward. The Holy Spirit is always calling us to Christ.

Isaiah 64:4 says, "For since the beginning of the world men have not heard, nor perceived by the ear, neither hath the eye seen, O God beside thee, what he hath prepared for him who waiteth for him."

He works in ways that are beyond our comprehension. Proverbs 3:5,6 says, "Trust in the Lord with all thine heart, and lean not unto thine own understanding. In all thy ways acknowledge him, and he shall direct thy paths."

Proverbs 16:19 says, "A man's heart deviseth his way, but the Lord directeth his steps."

There are many times when we don't know how to plan for success in this world where nothing seems to work right with any dependability because of evil, but God knows those who put their trust in Him. If you pray and trust, and do as you believe right, He will oversee your actions and keep your foot from slipping.

The spirit of prophecy is everywhere at all times. It is guiding us as individuals and as the body of Christ to accomplish the final will of God for us. When you are a Christian, your whole life is immersed in the spirit of prophecy. That spirit is the same as the Holy Spirit and He is here to work the will of God for us, both as individuals and as the church. Jesus, our appointed king, has come in a personal way to each one of us. He has suffered and died for us and is willing to accept us if we accept Him and acknowledge His authority. He has walked among us, endured the trials, temptation, and disappointments that we experience. He has lived in a world just as influenced and deceived by Satan as the one we live in today. He loves us and it is His ardent desire that we receive Him. But He is God, not just a sympathetic man, and will discipline us if we bring it on ourselves.

What do you imagine that He thinks of the way He is received in the United States today?

At the time I was born, the day of the week that we set aside to honor Christ was something you could notice. Business was closed and the churches were well attended. Preachers everywhere were preaching faithfully under the leadership of the Holy Spirit. This looked like a nation where our devotion to God made a difference. Marriages were committed and permanent. You could plainly see in our culture the ideal that parents were expected to instill responsibility and a way of thinking that was synonymous with Christian concepts in the children. The same was true in schools. What we saw in movies, heard on the radio, or read in books showed respect for Christian morals.

Look at the state of the nation now. Our children are robbed of the guidance of stable wisdom and prudence. Those who can afford it send their children to private schools because the public schools only excel in teaching a culture opposed to Christ, not basic education. Everywhere now in real life around them, and as portrayed in the media, children see a culture where marriage and Christian commitment of couples is no longer considered important.

They are encouraged now in our public institutions and the media to accept sexual perversion.

Addictive drugs are everywhere, being pushed on them at an early age. This is often conducted in well-organized cartels that operate with a cut going to some in law enforcement and the judiciary.

The churches in America should take note, especially the leaders and members of those that have forsaken the pure word of God and let in the voice of the one who is leading this world, of the words of Isaiah in 9:8 through 10:4.

> The Lord hath sent a word into Jacob, and it hath lighted upon Israel. And all the people shall know, even Ephraim and the inhabitant of Samaria, that say in the pride and stoutness of heart, the bricks are fallen down, but we will build with hewn stones; the sycamores are cut down, but we will change them into cedars.
>
> Therefore, the Lord shall set up the adversaries of Rezin against him and join in his enemies together; The Syrians before, and the Philistines behind, and they shall devour Israel with an open mouth.
>
> For all this his anger is not turned away, but his hand is stretched out still.
>
> For the people turneth not unto him who smiteth them, neither do they seek the Lord of hosts. Therefore, the Lord will cut off from Israel head and tail, branch and rush, in one day.
>
> The ancient and honorable, he is the head, and the prophet who speaketh lies, he

is the tail. For the leaders of this people cause them to err; and they who are led of them are destroyed. Therefore, the Lord shall have no joy in their young men, neither shall He have mercy on their fatherless and widows.

For all this His anger is not turned away, but His hand is stretched out still.

For wickedness burneth as the fire, it shall devour the briars and thorns, and shall kindle in the thickets of the forest, and they shall mount up like the lifting up of the smoke. Through the wrath of the Lord of hosts is the land darkened, and the people shall be as the fuel of the fire; no man shall spare his brother. And he shall snatch on the right hand and be hungry; and he shall eat on the left hand, and they shall not be satisfied. They shall eat every man the flesh of his own arm. Manasseh and Ephraim; and Ephraim and Manasseh; and they together shall be against Judah.

For all this his anger is not turned away, but his hand is stretched out still.

Woe unto them who decree unrighteous decrees, and who write grievousness which they have prescribed, to turn aside the needy from justice, and to take away the right from the poor of my people, that widows may be their prey, and that they may rob the fatherless! And what will ye do in the day of visitation, and in the desolation that will come from far? To whom will ye flee for help? And where will ye leave your glory? Without me they shall bow down under the prisoners, and they shall fall under the slain.

For all this his anger is not turned away, but his hand is stretched out still.

I believe this is true today; He is angry at what He sees, but His hand is stretched out still. I don't know how much time there is left but God wants His church to be doing all we can do to turn this nation around and I believe that if His people will get serious and work in the power of the Holy Spirit, we can see real revival.

But we can't do it quietly and timidly. The enemy is getting bolder every day. Just as big tech in social media is now beginning to censure, as disinformation, expressions not in alignment with the socialist agenda, or anything questioning them as fascist, so the day will come when fundamentalist Christian opinion will be labeled inappropriate for public expression.

I believe that we are now living in the latter days, but I also believe that if America will hear, accept the wisdom of Christ, and turn around we will be blessed, and if not, God's judgement will fall on the nation. He wants us to turn and be blessed, but He has to have someone to speak for Him. When God speaks to a nation, He speaks through His people. If He is to be heard, we have to let Him know that we want Him to be heard in earnest, and the Holy Spirit will use us in the spirit of prophecy as His voice. And if we, His church, will seek Him with the zeal that we should, He will make us a very convincing voice.

Chapter 16

Voices

Think about what we mean by a "voice" for the Lord. His voice is much more than a physical sound, it's a tremendous influence that can change the thoughts and course of action for the nation, or the world. Its purpose is reaching us with the mind of God and drawing us to Him. The "voice" is every conveyance the Lord uses for His thoughts and instructions toward us. Our continued prosperity or destruction depends on whether or not we hear and heed Him

God by His own design has put us in a world where we are exposed daily to two powers of voice. There is a voice in the world that tries to influence us with its tone to stir our emotions away from inner honesty and another that appeals to draw us to honesty, reasoning and responsibility.

We've all seen cartoons of a little devil, and a little angel perched on someone's shoulders with each one whispering in an ear. There is a lot of truth in that caricature because both God and the devil speak to us. In light of that, it will help you to better understand what's going on in the world by pondering the incredible power of the spiritual voices that gain our attention and how they work. The Bible uses the term "voice" to define the tremendous exertion of power and suggestion of both God and the evil spiritual realm in the world and how that power "speaks" to influence our actions.

When God created us to begin as carnal creatures, He supplied us with a physical voice so that the thoughts of our minds could be expressed to others. The voice was created so we could communicate and influence. In the bilateral world of the carnal and spiritual realm both God and the devil can and do use our voices to accomplish their purpose. God has spoken to men in an audible voice but both He and the devil usually speak to us through other people. God does it this way because He wants us to be like Him; free, responsible, and trustworthy because we have learned how to think, believe, and act out of experience and practice. The only way to do that is to speak to us, through us, and let the devil do the same. We just learn to be what He wants and commit to it our best through that experience.

We are different from all other of God's creatures. All others are finished work. We are not. He created us to become like Christ and the foundation for that has to be established in our own minds. We have to want to be this way of our own volition.

It is not possible for us to change from our present carnal nature to His under our own power, but we can be brought to want that. That is the purpose of God's voice, to draw us to Christ in earnest repentance and acknowledgement that His will for us is ours also. That change of heart has to come and it can't be just simply put there if we are to have the image of Christ.

Therefore, if there is another way you can choose to go, the voice for that must be allowed to speak so that the choice you make is of your own free will and a conscious commitment. We have to be exposed to both good and evil if we are to see the results and learn to choose the good. Thus, the greatest challenge to us as individuals and as the church of Christ is that the devil is allowed to freely try to distract us from God's voice and sell us a lie. He doesn't quit and must be opposed continually.

The Holy Spirit is the voice of God. We were designed and created to be like Him and His intended purpose for us is to move us along and mold us into Christ's likeness. He speaks to us with His voice, but if we refuse to hear Him, He still has the power to accomplish His final will and to subject us to anything He wants to achieve it, but He desires our cooperation for our own upbuilding. Deut. 8:5 says, "Thou shalt also consider in thine heart, that, as a man chasteneth his son, so the LORD thy God chasteneth thee."

Consider the history of His chosen people, Israel. They were under a covenant in which they agreed to hear and obey the voice of the Lord. The terms laid out in Deuteronomy 28:2 say, "And all these blessings shall come upon thee and overtake thee if thou shalt obey the voice of the Lord thy God." Deuteronomy 28:15 says, "But it shall come to pass, if thou wilt not hearken to the voice of the Lord thy God, to observe and to do all of His statutes which I command thee this day, that all these curses shall come upon thee and overtake thee;"

The curses written in that book happened. God offered the blessings, and they would have come if the people had obeyed. He had the power to make either happen, but they had to listen to His voice for the blessings to come. Because they didn't, for many centuries the nation of Israel ceased to exist as a land, but God kept His covenant, and the scattered people did not cease to exist. A remnant has always continued, and the entire history of Israel will play out exactly as God said.

If the voice of the Lord didn't have complete power to make His words come to pass there wouldn't be a person in the world today who knew that he had any Jewish ancestry or a resurrected state of Israel. In the long history of His chosen people, we see the awesome power of God's voice and serious consequences of not heeding. Proverbs 1:23-33 says,

> Turn ye at my reproof; behold, I will pour out my spirit unto you, I will makeknown my words unto you.
>
> Because I have called; and ye refused; I have stretched out my hand, and no man regarded, but ye have set at naught all my counsel, and would have none of my reproof, I also will laugh at your calamity; I will mock when your fear cometh; When your fear cometh as desolation, and your destruction cometh as a whirlwind; when distress and anguish come upon you.
>
> Then shall they call upon me, but I will not answer; they shall seek me early, but they shall not find me; because they hated

knowledge and did not choose the fear of the LORD.

They would have none of my counsel; they despised all my reproof. Therefore shall they eat of the fruit of their own way, and be filled with their own devices.

For the turning away of the simple shall slay them, and the prosperity of fools shall destroy them. But whoso hearkeneth to me shall dwell safely, and shall be quiet from fear of evil.

Like the nation of Israel, when anyone comes to God through Christ, he enters into a covenant which God has extended to him and agrees to hearken to His voice. God will discipline His children for our own good. He really wants to bless us, but He knows that we will become what He wants, only if, while free to examine our options, we choose to let Him in and hearken to His voice. To Hearken means to take seriously, honestly consider, and receive with reverence. This proverb describes what happens to those who don't. They reject His counsel and choose their own way over His. They will eat the fruit of their own way, and it will lead to their destruction. They will learn the hard way but those who fear Him will dwell safely without fear of evil.

When we confess Christ, we are confessing our own inadequacy but also that we are His personal children and now look to Him to lead us on the right pathway. When we do, He sends His Holy Spirit and He dwells within us. We then come to know and trust Him. We develop a real faith in Him, and this faith is the cornerstone of all that He is constructing in a Christian. Faith is personal. It establishes the real relationship that God wants to have with each of us, a personal knowledge that makes us give up the struggle that our vanities and insecurities bring so that we can hear His voice.

We also know that we can talk to Him and He listens. We let Him share our lives and development, teach us, and correct us. We can rest our spirits because we know we can trust Him with our future in a misled world.

The writer of Hebrews describes what happens when we heed His voice in that relationship, "There remaineth yet a rest to the people of God. For he that is entered into His rest, he hath also ceased from his own works, as God did from His. (Hebrews 4:9-10). Satan's deceptions lead to an unending vicious circle of work, fighting a mirage, and that work can never be completed. When we acknowledge Christ and surrender our lives to Him our relationship to Him becomes one of full trust and honesty about ourselves. He cannot be fooled and sees us exactly as we are but is faithful to lead us if we will trust Him. We then learn to see things in truth as He sees them, and we can rest in trust.

Hebrews 4:15-16 says, "For we have not an high priest who cannot be touched with feeling of our infirmities but was in all points tempted like as we are, yet without sin. Let us, therefore, come boldly unto the throne of grace, that we may obtain mercy, and find grace in time of need."

America is starving for this kind of personal relationship with our maker today. We need to know that there is someone in charge of things beyond our control who has our nature and cares about us. We need to know that he is a God that we can trust, who sees beyond our perceptions; a good Father, who already knows and provides what we need so that we don't have to invent our own salvation. This is truly a land in dire need of something that can give us this kind of rest and sense of direction we can trust. Everywhere we see a culture that is becoming ever crazier and more divergent. The days seem to be gone when we had confidence in God as our protector and guide. We're stressed out, trying to work our own work, and don't let God's rest in. We've become so rapt with conflicting voices of this world that we aren't hearing God's.

God speaks to us but allows us to be tempted and tried for our own good. If we refuse to hear His voice there is no way left for us to learn but by eating the fruit of our own devices, and He will let us if we insist. But if we are willing to confess Christ and put our trust in Him, He will lead us like a father. We are unable to complete His work in us without Him but when we confess Christ, he resides in us to finish it. When God's work is finished Satan's will be destroyed and we are destined to become spiritual creatures like the risen Christ. If we let Him do His work in us, we will know His voice. and will also shun the voice that contradicts Him. That is a pretty good summation of the work of the church, to serve as the vehicle through which God speaks to bring us all to a personal knowledge and relationship with Christ so that we know His voice.

To be the vehicle for the voice of God is a very serious responsibility in a world where the devil also speaks freely. We don't become Christians by just sitting down and thinking everything through ourselves. We become Christians by hearing the voice of God.

Chapter 17

The Duty of The Church

I f you want people to perceive things and think the way you want, you have to make the voice for your side be heard. Simply put, the devil's side is doing a much better job than the church. The church was formed for the purpose of bringing God's voice to the world. We are supposed to be indoctrinating the world to hear God's voice and keep ourselves united and on track to heed it also. (Matthew 5:13-16; 24:14; 28:18-20)

It's the duty of the church to bring to the world's attention the dangers and foolishness of Satan's misguidance and the wisdom of hearing and heeding the Holy Spirit and God promises to give us power if we will try.

"But ye shall receive power after the Holy Spirit is come upon you; and ye shall be witness unto me both in Jerusalem, and in all Judea, and in Samaria, and unto the uttermost part of the Earth." Acts 1:8

We can't expect the people to receive Christ if His word is not brought to them. Neither can we expect them to grow in understanding and develop the wisdom and strength to resist the powerful voice of Satan if the church is not preaching and explaining the voice of God. Our Lord has to be able to reach people just like the devil. He has to be shown in a favorable light and be continually heard to implant the foundation for His way of thinking in us.

Both God and the devil must employ some of the methods of the modern propagandist to reach people. That is what the entire spiritual war is about, teaching people to think the way the voice wants. Each has a strategy for capturing and conditioning minds and a plan for building a culture that provides the best atmosphere to empower their voice.

The foundation of God's plan is Jesus. He is changing you to think and believe the way you were intended to from the beginning; to prepare you to be a spirit creature who will live forever as a part of God's Family in perfect peace, love, and harmony. He wants to lead you to a clear and deep understanding of the nature of the spirit person He has prepared you to be, as well as how the carnal nature you now have prevents you from being that. The only way He can lead you into the path of eternal life and spiritual wisdom is to lead you to Himself. You can't do it by yourself, you have to come to Him in trust. To draw you into this relationship He has done three things.

First, He has shown that He is completely committed to us by living a life on earth as a man. He did this subjecting Himself to every temptation and limitation of power that we face. He followed His own rules and precepts that He had set for us, even to a cruel, horrible death on a cross while those that Satan had fooled mocked and taunted, and He finished it all sinless.

Next, having done this, He completely justified Himself and established His right to authority. You cannot say that He is insincere in wanting to help you.

Third, when you confess Him, He gives you the Holy Spirit to dwell within you. The spirit speaks directly to you and by inspiration through others to put and keep you on the right path. All that Christ does for us is done through the power of the Holy Spirit.

The Spirit established the church. The Church is here to receive His direction and proclaim His voice; to teach us how to think, act, and believe to be blessed by His work. We, as individuals, and the church collectively, have the Holy Spirit.

It is important, though, that you never forget that this is a personal relationship. No one is responsible for the group. You are responsible for yourself directly to Jesus. Each Christian has the duty to act on behalf of the Church by following the Spirit in faith and publicly supporting the things of Christ. That is how Jesus acted in His life as a man on earth as an example for us.

If you believe in Jesus, you have to believe in the duty of the Church to take His voice through the Holy Spirit to the world. God means for the church to be dedicated, active, and led by the Holy Spirit.

What is the message entrusted to the church? It is that when God made us to live in a carnal state, subject to evil temptation, He did it with a plan. He promises that if we will have faith in Christ. He will bring us to a new state through death and resurrection in a new spiritual body. In this state we will all be open and sinless; seeing and willing to be seen exactly as we are. We will live forever in the light of His presence in a world where sin is overcome, and all is peace and bliss. Our journey begins with repenting of sin and inviting Christ in to direct our lives, entrusting our final fate to Him alone. He will be with us throughout our whole journey and will not forsake us. Our destiny is to have His nature.

The Christian life is all about God with us. It's not about love of a philosophy or an organization. It's about the love of a person. You can't be a half-hearted or lukewarm Christian. There is only one right response to what He has done for us, and it is the duty of the church and every believer to love Him and help bring this message of salvation though a personal relationship to all. There is no point in Jesus suffering the things He did for us if it is not going to be told to the world and no one but us is going to do it.

Like God, the devil also has an agenda and a strategy to draw us under his influence. I can tell you what God's agenda is because He makes it clear, but Satan's is somewhat murkier, He may have once thought that if he could lead us away from God, he could become some sort of god or king to us? (Isaiah 14:13) Unlike Jesus, He has no personal affection for you. He has never shown that he would be willing to suffer a stubbed toe for you, much less the agony of death on a cross. He doesn't think of you as being like him and doesn't want you to have any spiritual power because he couldn't trust you. His entire purpose in dealing with us seems to be to try to convince God that we are not worth what He is doing for us.

I don't know whether he ever really thought there was any gainful purpose in his pursuits or not. All I can tell you is that when Jesus gasped His final words on the cross, the devil knew he had lost. The only thing he can hope to accomplish now is to spite Jesus by showing Him how easily we are led to ignore him.

He wants to lead you on a path that will keep you away from the personal commitment and responsibility that the Holy Spirit gives by appealing to your carnal nature. He knows that he must keep you away by attempting to destroy every channel that God uses to reach you and keep you from thinking about the message of wisdom in God's voice. He knows that it is easy to lead our carnal nature to minimize reasoning and spiritual responsibility. If he can keep you from truth, he can convolute your reasoning.

How many persons today who are kept away from the voice of God would say that they can't believe that a God who loves us would send anyone to hell. Yet doesn't it make sense that heaven is prepared for a people who will have the mindset to keep it sinless? You can't get there just ignoring the voice of Christ who was willing to die for you on a cross. Do you think Jesus doesn't know what is required to make Heaven work? Do you think Satan is going to Heaven?

What Jesus offers is the most valuable thing in the universe and what Satan gives is the most frighteningly dreadful. A lot of us may have some picture formed in our minds of hell being a place where those there are tormented in a way that we can be cruelly treated here. But can anything be worse than not receiving the new body Christ gives and spending forever in darkness with only your thoughts in the company of Satan and those who chose Satan over

Christ, away from the light of His presence? Matthew 8:12, 22:13, 25:30)

We all want our freedom and cannot be forced to think one way or another. But one way leads to everlasting joyful life, and the other to eternal misery. The two cannot coexist forever, and which way we choose depends on which voice we heed. The duty of the church to take God's voice to the world is very serious. If we don't, millions will suffer eternal consequences that they were kept unaware of. We have to realize that it is our duty to invade the culture that the devil wants to prevail and take it back for the Lord, not just stay on our side of the battle line.

Chapter 18

Effects From the Wrong Voice

I t is amazing how the devil can completely corrupt us by degrees when he can lead us away from the voice of God.

Look at the ways noted earlier that we're being led away from God. Think about the psychology being applied, the results, how each gain the devil makes weakens our resistance to the next, and how he incorporates each result into an overall plan.

Earlier I mentioned that the way most of the modern media operates evolved from ideas conceived by the Fabian Society. Again, I'm sure everyone who participated in its formulation saw themselves as doing a good thing that would change human society for the better. This occurred in the early days of the industrial revolution when some of the wealthiest enterprisers were amassing huge fortunes at the expense of the long, hard labor of many less fortunate who received little for it.

Concern for the compassionate treatment of the less fortunate and treating all as equal in worth is certainly not an unchristian way of thinking. I'm sure they all really believed that the final result would only be a new world in which all would be better provided for, and we would all be of a sounder, healthier frame of mind. They never saw that the devil would weave his corrupting influence into their plans the way he has.

But, without seeking the voice of God, they became fascinated with their own designs and unwittingly let the devil take over their work. They let pride convince them that they were a supranational intellectual community, destined to save and bring the world to societal maturity with their own scheming devices. In time, what began as a plan to develop propaganda as a social science and change western culture to socialism in steps developed into a plan for worldwide indoctrination to create a completely new agnostic culture and way of thinking.

As they broadened the scope of their plan, they became mesmerized that they had the power to surreptitiously change the entire world into a single, one-world, secular culture by subtly destroying all existing religions, cultural practices, and other perceived barriers by degrees. In doing so they also were rejecting and opposing the voice of God, choosing their own way over his and their intellectual pride over real empathy for others.

Look where it led. The use of propaganda to control our minds and our political, social and cultural orientation has become a total obsession with the heirs of the Fabian mindset in total disregard for truth and fair representation of other viewpoints. We've seen collusion with them in the highest reaches of our legislative and justice departments to create illusions to advance their agenda and damage their opposition. It seems that the more profligate our society becomes and the more deceptive the media becomes, the more persistent and determined they become to lead us farther in the same direction.

The society they are creating is just the opposite of the utopian ideal they project in their imagery. Their agenda to move us toward socialism is based on trickery and deceit. They create the illusion that all resistance to them is seen as hatred and bigotry, and it results in a resentful, divided society. They are really just disobeying the Lord's command to not bear false witness, and the result is the fruit of following their own way, described in the proverb.

Many Americans now feel that we're living in a society under the control of an all-powerful voice that daily chides us with no way to make ours heard. We feel oppressed continually by the domineering spectral influence of a society that is determined to crush and force us to confess that what we don't believe is so. We've become more divided, expecting no fair treatment from the voice, which we see as the image of our society, and respond by giving none. We've become distracted from the responsibility to put God's rules first as our moral guide. Instead, to fight back, we've adopted the mindset of the voice ourselves and we, as a nation, are becoming morally bankrupt, distrustful of each other, and unable to be a cohesive force.

There is now a wider gap between rich and poor in America. There are more drug addicts, more homeless people, more mental illness, and more crime. The cost of identity theft and other white-collar crimes, as well as plain old shoplifting, runs into mind boggling billions. Scams are rampant.

Liberal news agencies have almost taken all control of the campaigning period before elections to eliminate honest debate of the issues and destroy their opposition with smears, manipulations, and creating situations to inspire distrust and hatred.

The entertainment industry, newscasting, public education, and many schools of higher learning now reflect the godless, secular culture to be the norm. Underneath the glory and glamor they portray for a society that has rejected Gods' emphasis on sexual morality, family structure, and following Christ, we see the real picture of a nation in serious decline into misery and emptiness.

Suicide among teenagers has reached a shocking rate. Mass shootings with no motive other than just a general rage against the society around us are becoming regular news events. The crime rate in the inner cities has exploded, especially murder. The welfare system has resulted in a huge number of children growing up in fatherless homes; dependent on the system for survival, and with no one to teach responsibility. Drug trafficking and gang violence are taking over. More policemen are dying in the line of duty and law breakers are becoming more brazen to resist arrest or threaten officers.

In this environment the police are often called into crime ridden inner city areas to make arrests in violent and dangerous situations but are hesitant to give more than minimum presence and protection. If an incident ever results in a white policeman shooting a black man, it takes over the news as a racist crime with the liberal media conjuring a national outpouring of sympathy for the criminal and the policeman being tried and condemned to prison in the news.

No one in the news really cares about the criminal as a person. His case only becomes a national obsession as a distracting tool to deter any shift toward populism in America and label anyone opposed to them as a racist. The end result of this well-orchestrated scheme is that we now have fewer policemen and more crime and murder in the inner cities. The very thing that bred crime before has proliferated and the children there are in an atmosphere even worse. What these neighborhoods really need is Christian homes with responsible Christian fathers serving as role models and teachers to the children.

We're seeing an aimless, frustrated attitude and pattern of behavior in every element of America youth on a path to senseless ruin with heartbroken parents and an older generation in utter dismay and it is getting worse, not better.

The reason for this is simple. We have not heeded God's voice. If Satan can convince us that God's voice is not important on one point, he is poised and ready to take us step by step to abandoning Him completely.

Look again at the sexual revolution of the 1960's and all of its results. The voice of God is very clear and makes perfect sense. He has given us plain instructions for sexual morality and family structure. The bond of marriage and the marriage bed are sacred. When men and women respect His wisdom and apply His guidelines it makes a world of difference from what we are seeing now.

When we usurp the right to have sexual relations with whoever is a willing partner and then decide if we want to live with them, we are seeing them more as a sexual object than an objective look at whether they are the right person to commit to and will commit to us, or if they will fulfill the responsibility of parenthood. Decisions are made solely on the basis of whether your partner makes you feel good; First, are they a good sex partner and second, is there something about them that just makes you feel good when you are with them.

No doubt, these are desirable things to have in a good marriage but when we go about things our way instead of God's we are only looking to satisfy our own ego, and the end result will not be good; not to us personally or to us as a society. We are turning the nature of our carnal bodies, which will soon grow old and die, into our god instead of the one who guides us on the safe path of eternal life. Our society will eventually crumble because we rejected Him and would have none of His reproof. When we cease to practice God's ways ourselves, we're certainly not going to pass them on to the next generation.

There is a good reason for God's stress on sexual morality, marriage, and the duty of husbands, wives, and children in the family relationship. It's about children. What they become depends on committed family life. Children, at the earliest ages when they begin to think and observe, are not looking inward or upward, they are looking outward. There is nothing yet formed inward, especially with no spiritual connection. They begin learning by imitation. A child of that age means no harm but has no sense of responsibility.

He only has a sense of belonging. Before he knew anything someone took care of him, and as he began to develop and became aware of his surroundings, there was someone to whom he belonged. He also developed a sense that others his age belonged to their parents and his sense of identity with his parents and family put him in a psychological realm from which there is no escape. Hopefully, he finds this a good haven, not a bad confinement. But either way there is no escape. His subconscious mind is locked into it, and he sees his parents as part of a fate over which they have control and with which others will identify him. The parents are the only security that a young child has, and that factor is an inextricable element in his development.

Young children beginning to develop will idolize their parents and try to be like them by imitation. As they grow and interact with others, they come to realize that the parents are not the perfect role models they once believed. The past pattern of imitation can turn to inner feelings of ambivalence, disillusionment, or at worst embarrassment and resentful anger. God has given us in His word the best way to cope with this unavoidable factor, but it is still one of the greatest challenges we face as parents or children growing up. It is a lesson in open honesty that parents must learn and practice themselves and teach to the children.

Parents may be aware that they have a duty to guide children but may not really be aware of how much this is a two-way street. Children are also subconsciously aware that the parents are responsible for their development. As they grow, they will never learn to look inward or upward without guidance. It is almost impossible to develop personal responsibility and honesty with oneself without good teaching and it won't be done if the parents are not hearing the voice of God.

The bible tells us to teach children by precept and example. When parents do that, it benefits not only the children, but themselves as well, and therefore, society as a whole. When parents are trying to teach that way, precept has to be explained. To teach personal responsibility to children requires honesty. To explain the reasoning, you must be willing to admit your own susceptibility to temptation and failure. You can't develop this character trait without having an honest awareness that the weakness exists in everyone, and neither can you teach it without that, and a real consciousness that you should try to live up to the standard you're trying to instill in them.

Without this, children will only become increasingly frustrated, angry, and rebellious as they grow toward maturity. What should be a good sense of having a family to belong to will be subliminally perceived as a barrier of subjugation they can't escape. Without it, if you are a good example they will be subconsciously angry that you haven't taught them the confidence to be so themselves, and if you aren't, they will see you as a hypocrite who rules over them, and rebel against your authority. Put simply, they have to be told the truth and made to understand our sin nature to be able to cope with it.

Growing up in this world can be a frightening experience and everyone needs to be taught how to deal with the challenges we face. We can't teach children everything they need to know but when we apply God's word to our family life, we teach them how to deal with feelings of inadequacy and insecurity. These are a natural part of life, and it is human nature to let the voice of Satan lead us to blame someone else for our lack of confidence and perseverance when facing the unknown. The way of wisdom and faith through knowing yourself and God has to be taught.

Satan now has a milieu where children trying to be Christians can no longer feel accepted. It is extremely difficult for parents trying to raise children by Christian principles if they are in a society that ignores God. We can never give America's children what they need for healthy mental and spiritual development until we change back to a Christian culture. Children are discouraged if they feel they have an identity forced on them as part of a tiny minority in a world where Satan's ways are accepted in high regard and God's ways are seen as old fashioned and peculiar.

This is the world in which children are growing up today. All around them they see premarital sex as an accepted and expected part of our culture, men and women living together unwed, trying to avoid the unwanted responsibility of children, sensual pleasure glorified, and Christian family values minimized.

America today is in desperate need of the voice of God and our children are abandoned to the voice of the world. This tragic development goes back to the sexual revolution of the 1960's, and its acceptance facilitated the way for Satan to simultaneously corrupt us away from God in the next steps.

Chapter 19

Why The Devil Uses the Left

The devil is always working his voice in fervently to confuse and mislead our culture away from heeding the voice of God and making us believe that what we're doing is progressive and best for the current situation. The best way for him to do that is to so overwhelm us with earthly challenges and the guiding tone of his own voice that we are so distracted we obsess and act on our own, not taking time to seek the voice of God. His opportunity to distract the church was greatly expanded in the era that was beginning a little before I was born.

At the end of World War II, the greatest perceived threat to world peace suddenly became the communist dictatorship of the Soviet Union. They immediately took over the bordering countries of eastern Europe, extended their influence in eastern Asia, and attempted to foment takeovers in various other parts of the world. We were suddenly in the age of nuclear weapons and the threat of the complete destruction of a divided world seemed very real.

We felt ourselves extremely pressured as the world's most powerful nation to diplomatically keep a world of different creeds from falling to the tyranny of communism. We, as a nation, were new to this role and the voice of the devil rang out loud and clear that his way was the only fair way.

Socialist propagandists took full advantage of this situation to hype the picture of an impartial nation that holds all creeds equal as being our noblest ideal. That clearly implies is that none, including Christianity, are sufficient to be one's moral determinant but their way is. The voice of the devil has cultivated this until today it seems that American government holds as its highest aspiration the total avoidance of any appearance of any Christian motivations. All he had to do was be persistent with the same theme, that politeness and consideration require that we always give deference to the pride of the world over Christ to not be offensive to anyone.

In the never-ending war of Satan's voice against God's, he turns us every which way but loose. He will have you completely focused on one enemy while he is getting another more dangerous one, right here among us.

When I was in the sixth grade our teacher was teaching a geography lesson one day and the threat of a communist takeover in southeastern Asia came up. One of our classmates asked in a seriously inquisitive tone, "What is communism?" It became apparent that a lot of the class didn't know what the ideological concept was.

Our teacher then explained, as I remember roughly, that there was no private ownership of business, and everyone received the same thing. The immediate surprised reaction of several was, "What's wrong with that?'

Our teacher went on to explain in a way that I believe left most of us thinking that ours really was a system that worked better. But the fact that so many at that age were shocked to learn that our nation was opposed to something they automatically thought of as fair treatment and our ideal of equality should tell you something about the reach of the voice they'd been hearing, and that was in 1954 or 55.

The motive of communism is to change the way people think away from individualism and personal responsibility to collectivism. Everyone is to think of himself as a member of the group and the group is the whole human race. Communist ideology recognizes that we don't naturally think that way now and must be forced to change by making us live in a dictatorial system where we have to practice collectivism until we are completely indoctrinated by propaganda; in other words, the communist government must be the "voice" that changes us from heeding personal conscience to conforming to group attitude.

To be a complete communist you must not think of yourself as a member of the family of your birth, but rather the collective family. All religion, cultural differences, and anything that pulls you away from collectivist culture toward individualism must be destroyed. The collectivist culture becomes your god.

Like communism, socialism also seeks to change our way of thinking as a "voice" through propaganda. They also believe that the world is destined towards a single universal culture with all religion and cultural differences done away with. But, unlike communism, they strive to keep moving the world toward that goal in a free society by using propaganda to undermine and destroy original cultural or religious concepts, conjuring constant negative imagery about their opposition, and serving as the spin doctor for secularism and collectivist thinking.

Their strategy is to attempt to control, as much as possible without using dictatorial forces, every available means of communication through a deliberate, coordinated effort of like-minded people. Thus, they become a powerful voice for socialism in a free society, changing the national mindset to think in a more collectivist manner.

This is done by focusing matters of conscience and responsibility on a group. Nothing is changed by reason and debate or appeal to individual conscience. It is done by creating a mental picture of good and bad group attitudes and exposing us all to a daily barrage of accusatory propaganda.

This is the difference in the voice of the Holy Spirit and the voice of the world. The Holy Spirit appeals to the individual conscience of each person. The implication is that you need to do something and that something about you needs to be changed.

A new convert, drawn to Christ under the convicting power of the Holy Spirit is asked by an evangelist to pray some version of the "sinner's prayer." Essentially, you say to the Lord that you are a sinner, repent, and ask Him to come into your life and save you from sin. No blame is placed on others, you just admit that you are a sinner in a sinful world.

When coming to Christ we are confessing and repenting of sin in complete honesty and can no longer use the attitude of ourselves or others as an excuse. We know that He sees us just as we are and are asking for mercy, not justice. When we do this, we have to realize the awesome power that

Satan has held over us. Without Jesus, none of us would ever overcome sin on his own and He is taking us while we are still sinners. We can't come to Him without a deep sense of our failure at personal responsibility and how much we owe to Him. Personal responsibility is a necessary part of a strong cohesive society, and it is a habit that has to be learned and practiced. When socialist propaganda focuses on group behavior instead, the implication is that the attitude of a group is held in collective approval or contempt, and all you need to do is be sure your attitude aligns with the one held in approval. Thus, individual responsibility and reason is minimized, and you are conditioned to be led without resistance.

Socialist propaganda has created an idol in their mental image of the modern, well informed, and well-adjusted person as one who will promote the socialist agenda. He is portrayed as one who has fully adopted the socialist conjecture of political correctness as the modern standard of true morality. He is the well-received paragon of well-intentioned and balanced people everywhere; one who truly "has it all together." He is aware, knowledgeable, and indeed intellectually appreciative of the role that cultural differences have played in shaping our world. But he is aware that there is a growing consensus everywhere, as the world matures and draws closer, that all religion was created in the minds of men in a more isolated and less enlightened time. He is fully aware, and the progressive element of humanity everywhere agrees, that our future lies in a socialist world where men have cast aside the superstitious inhibitions of religion and are joining together in the bonds of secular human wisdom. He is confident that progressive minded people everywhere are coming to the same outlook and believes that as our world heads toward full maturity it will be restructured by these concepts.

This glorified image is as much an idol as a statue of Baal. An idol is something the devil uses to convince us that there is a way to curry the favor of an unseen spiritual force other than hearing and obeying the voice of God. No idol worshipper ever thought that a carved or molten image was a god. He thought that a spiritual force that could be harnessed to satisfy his carnal desires could be reached through the image.

The difference in that idol spirit and God is what is required of us. The idol may require a sacrifice to show that you are sincere with him, but never any self-examination. God requires that you be honest with both Him and yourself. The idol never requires anything that causes friction with the secular culture or that the carnal nature is not already tempted to do.

Using this old psychological trick is how the devil was able to turn so many to the idolatry of secularism after the sexual revolution of the 1960's. We know that the Holy Spirit requires honesty when we come to Him and when we know that God is not pleased with us, we will either turn back to Him in sincerity and change our ways or try to run away from facing Him. If we become hooked on the devil's ways and want that more than living God's way, we go away from Him because we cannot be honest with ourselves in His presence. The left provides the picture of a different set of rules for right and wrong we use to deny guilt and justify ourselves when we let ourselves be lured into the devil's lifestyle. There aren't many of us who don't have the power of reasoning to understand that following God's rules will keep us strong and safe both as individuals and as a society, but there are many who will run from the truth and listen to the voice that tells them what they'd rather hear.

The psychology behind this is the devil's oldest trick. He used it on Adam and Eve to bring sin into the world, on Israel to turn them to idol worship, and he is using it to corrupt America's culture and destroy the church today.

Chapter 20

Preach Christ

The devil understands the human psyche better than any trained psychologist and he knows how to open and shut each door for us so the church will destroy itself from within. He knows that after each victory he accomplishes to pull us another step from the voice of God, we will create an excuse and get used to it. Every strategy he has pursued; the destruction of family, giving deference to the world's ideas over God's, the idolatrous glorification of secular culture, directing our focus away from personal responsibility to group attitude, are all leading to the ultimate goal; to erase Christ from our minds.

All these things prepare our attitudes for the total elimination of "fundamentalist" Christianity which is meant to be the final destruction of the church. With every giving of ground to secularism the church becomes a little more complacent and our carnal nature to excuse ourselves a little stronger. Our focus shifts from the spiritual to the world.

This is what progressively happens; we pay less attention to the voice of God and more to the devil. We begin to replace the words of God with what comes from our natural desire to be held in approval and recreate in our minds a God who is satisfied with us. Eventually the god we need to excuse ourselves is so much in conflict with the God of Christ that we have to push Christ out entirely. The god we're left with only created the universe from which we evolved. He has left it to us to create our own code of ethics as we evolve.

He might be willing to help us out in a pinch, but requires nothing of us, doesn't act as a counselor, or try to direct our thoughts and behavior. We, of course, are not going to give much thought to Heaven in our busy schedules, but we know He loves and understands us and will certainly see to it that we go there.

The culture that Satan has created in America has been working new inroads into this final apostasy now for decades. The attack on fundamentalist thought is now on fertile ground.

Our conception of America has shifted from a people who used our freedom to pursue what we personally saw as right, to the world's most powerful state with an urgent onus to use this power to bring a world of differing cultures and creeds to accept and cooperate with each other and steer us in into a more homogeneous world. Secular propaganda portrays the fundamentalist belief of the Church as a barrier to that; an uncooperative element with a mule-headed stubbornness that others see as a defiant disdain of their basic rights and dignity; a people who can't interact fairly with others because of a blind and senseless fixation on a set of outdated rules that are based on fiction and folk-lore and have no relevance to current affairs.

This deception has already worked its way into many of the mainstream seminaries and other bases of influence to undermine belief in the fundamentals of the faith and turn out preachers and writers who question the authority of scripture. Many of the mainstream churches were intim-idated to change to a softer image that they thought would appeal to a nation of changing religious outlook. A new gen-eration of Americans began to hear a message that sounded more like a calling to political correctness than an appeal to hear the voice of God. They were cleverly conned to accept the voice of the world over God's.

This has taken a heavy toil. We are now into the third generation of this new era and everywhere we see a nation that is losing all spiritual wisdom and being drawn into complete secular insanity. If this trend is not reversed it will be the end of most churches in America.

The reversal needed can begin in the pulpits of some of the mainstream churches with the realization that you've been misled. You naturally believed that when you enrolled in seminary the purpose was to prepare you with more knowledge and understanding to make you more effective, but some are doing just the opposite.

Let me elaborate by citing something I read in a Methodist quarterly thirty-some years ago. The writer described the suffering-servant passages in Isaiah 52:13 through 53:12 as a tribute to some unnamed person who had suffered unjustly for his people. He concluded by saying that the passages remind Christians of the sufferings of Christ.

The idea being conveyed by many liberal Bible teachers is that Isaiah was compiled from a number of sources to create a consolidation of real and imagined historical folklore to give the Jews a sense of identity and unity. All this is doing is leading you away from the voice of God, the Holy Spirit.

The entire conception and context of the Christian faith is that God created us to be spiritual creatures and we're being led to completion through Christ and the calling of the Holy Spirit. He speaks to us!

This is being undermined by the liberal Bible teachers. Much of what they say creates doubts to lead you away from letting the Holy Spirit give you the power and authority to preach the true gospel of Christ effectively.

Look at the passages from Isaiah again. They begin by saying that my (God's) servant *shall deal prudently and be exalted and high.* He still lives and His work isn't finished yet. When He was beaten beyond recognition it *would sprinkle many nations.* He has *borne our griefs and carried our sorrows.* Verse 5 is very plain, *He was bruised for our iniquities, and the chastisement for our peace was upon Him.* Verse 6 says *that the Lord has laid on Him the iniquity of us all.* Verse 10 says *that it pleased the Lord to bruise Him and He made His soul an offering for sin.*

These words are about Christ, not some unnamed or possibly unreal person. They are the words given by the Holy Spirit to Isaiah centuries before it happened.

Jesus affirmed the inspiration of Isaiah. At the beginning of His ministry, He read from Isaiah 61:1-2 in the synagogue and said that these words were fulfilled in their ears that day. All that He ever said about the scriptures confirmed that He held them to be inspired and true.

I believe that a lot of preachers today have received the kind of training that will only make them keep people away from the full gospel message of the Holy Spirit. Without His leadership the people will revert more and more to the devices of their own imaginations and the church will evolve into weaker commitment until it dies.

That can turn around if they will realize that false teachings have kept them from the full arsenal of God and recognize the reality and purpose of the Holy Spirit. Realize that he speaks through you, and not to address worldly issues, but to reach the spirit within us. He will then supply you and use you to bring His word and presence. The creeping apostasy and desertion we're now seeing can turn to revival.

God provided what you need in the Bible. The bible's purpose is to make us hear and understand His voice. The voice of the enemy wants to make us lose interest and stop reading the Bible because we believe it isn't true from a historical or inspirational perspective so he can rework our perception of Jesus as only a man; an influential Rabbi who was turned on and persecuted by the religious establishment of his day for teaching an enlightened version of Jewish faith that was much the same as modern political correctness.

It then becomes easy to live the new, imagined Christian life. Little thought and no self-examination are called for and sin is not a real problem. God is satisfied with us, just as we are, and no personal relationship is called for.

Jesus didn't come to earth as a radical new teacher. He is the author of the law and came to fulfill it, not to change or reinterpret it. He taught that sin is serious and will keep you out of Heaven. He came to live a sinless life and to be the perfect sacrifice for our sins. He was a teacher, but much more. He is the Son of God, and if we take away His divinity, we take away our indebtedness. He is no longer central with any compelling claim to our allegiance and the church will eventually die.

What the liberal element of the church today is doing is trying to convince us that the Bible may not be true from a historical standpoint but there is still social value in some of the thoughts expressed in it. This kind of church won't last another generation.

This kind of church is all about social consciousness without the voice of God. The church is certainly called to have a social conscience but if it is not led by the Holy Spirit its' social conscience will eventually digress into what we are now seeing in America. In the early days the Methodist Church, for example, was a church of social consciousness and supported social action toward a more equitable society, but it was led by the Holy Spirit. The first devotion of the members was to Christ and the duty to bring the gospel to the world. We are called by the spirit as individuals with a personal consciousness and when we have a society of personally responding people, we have a right social consciousness for the nation.

When you look at how Satan has lured us away from Christ by degrees in my lifetime you may wonder in awe if we can ever resist the master plan of such an evil genius. Satan, though, is not a strategic genius at spiritual warfare. Every move he has made is based on one simple trick. It's the same one he used on Adam and Eve.

He knows that our carnal nature makes us want to not admit fault when we go against God's word and he knows that our carnal nature still tempts us, keeping us subliminally aware of our guilt. Like Adam and Eve, we want to hide from God and justify ourselves by blaming someone or something else for our failure. That justification we seek is always through attitude. We are not guilty because our attitude is really good, so whoever caused us to sin must have the attitude of deliberate sin and we are guiltless. If you'll look back at history from creation to now, you'll see that Satan has used this same trick on everyone he ever led away, and in America today he's harnessing the same thing to keep us from seeing the seriousness of our sin or our need to have it covered by Christ.

The devil has worked out his plan to destroy our morals and culture, most ostensibly through the socialist movement. But socialism is not what is really destroying us and turning us into socialists is not his goal. The ploy he uses to destroy us is to convince the manipulators of socialist strategy that we need to be steered away from the voice of God.

In spite of the incessant voice we hear in news, entertainment, education, and every other venue that can be used as a tool, we are not really becoming socialists. Nobody is really trying to teach us the basics of socialist economics or cultural theory. The devil simply has their strategists convinced that God must be eliminated and replaced with a prevailing attitude and then we will just naturally become a socialist society.

We're not becoming socialists, we're just becoming a people who ignore the voice of God and the personal, responsible, relationship we have with Him. We're adopting, instead, an attitude that the devil can control in us.

Many in America's churches todays are distracted by the daily accusatory voice of Satan and are so absorbed by it that they respond just the way he wants. We are constantly exposed to a barrage of socialist propaganda and stand accused of being fascists, racists, or hatemongers if we oppose. Satan wants us so preoccupied that we feel we must inwardly respond by making sure our attitude is aligned in passive approval and are thus not guilty and so, are right with our imaginary god.

Some churches are leading themselves into apostacy today because they seem to be losing the younger generation and try to attract them back by many devices other than preaching the truth of God's voice. The church is meant to be a place of fellowship and a source of help in our daily living, but we will accomplish nothing by changing the message we send those who are choosing their own way over God's. If we change the church to compromise with the devil's voice we are working for the devil, not God. Our purpose is to bring the voice of Christ to the world through the power of the Holy Spirit.

Step back and look at how the devil has changed the disposition of American culture during my lifetime. Eighty years ago, the basic Christian concepts of morality were firmly embedded in our mentality. Children were called down and disciplined by parents for going along with the crowd instead of acting responsibly. The motivation of our national concept was to provide and keep an aura where God's values, wisdom, and voice prevailed.

Now the devil has overwhelmed us, turning us around from the ideal of each person using freedom to be the best he can to staying silent while the crowd leads. He did this simply by using the same trick on us that he used on Adam and Eve and being persistent. He has used every resource from school textbooks to the daily news to imbed in our minds that the way to fix our problems is with attitude, not a relationship with God. Have the right attitude and go with the flow! That is done by simply having it spoken of as if it were just an obvious and accepted fact every day. His voice has become such an ever present, pervasive fata morgana in our daily lives that it doesn't occur to us that there is any way but his to deal with our problems, or that he created them in the first place.

Is he not doing the same thing in America's churches? Many preachers today are under pressure to deal with people deserting the church by trying to present the gospel in a way that would seem more appealing to the way the secular culture leads them to think. This only creates confusion, less interest in your message, and ultimately alienates you from both the world and the Holy Spirit. You can't modify or negate the role of the church He suffered and died to establish and expect any help from Him. Jesus came into the world to bring the voice of God, not to argue or negotiate with the devil.

If we want to not become ensnared in the devil's wiles, we have to completely trust and be devoted to the Holy Spirit, like the church used to be, and He will show us the right path. He will provide us with the voice that builds personal responsibility, fellowship, and real concern for each other and away from a simple attitude of hatred for one group and approval for another. We have to let God use the church for His voice and restore the culture that respects God.

That is the main difference in the strong, vibrant church of the past and the church of today. They realized that they were in a spiritual warfare of voices and had the duty to oppose the devil while lifting up the voice of the Holy Spirit. When people hear Christ preached under the compelling power of the Holy Spirit they feel the compulsion to faithfully attend and support the church. That is why they were powerful and respected while the modern church is weak and dying. If we want the church revived, we have to be like the old church again. They stayed focused and realized what the enemy was up to.

Every preacher should stay aware that the devil will use everything he can to fool the church and the nation, and that includes you. What is heard from you is assumed to represent the voice of God, and if you are deceived it will deceive others. Be aware that the devil is very subtle and crafty. He is always trying to lure those who have influence over you to fool you into thinking that you are serving God when you are really serving him. Know the voices and be sure that the Holy Spirit is the only one heard coming from your pulpit. Preach Christ faithfully and leave the results of your work to God. It may seem like not many want to hear it now, but He is able to bring the day when they will realize they do.

Chapter 21

Where Are We Now?

Look around at our world today in light of Bible prophecy. When God revealed to Moses what would happen to Israel, He offered the chance to hearken to His voice and said that they would be scattered if they didn't. He also said that in the latter days they would be brought back home. To the church He warned of the false teachings that would cause our love of Christ to cool and said that in the last days the deception would grow stronger.

Now the nation of Israel is reestablished, but they are still not a people on fire for God and many do not attend the synagogue on the Sabbath. We also see the spirit of antichrist taking over many of the mainstream churches. Attendance is falling off and many are now ignoring the authority of God's word and teaching secular ideas that ignore and spite our Lord to His face. The Holy Spirit is contradicted daily with false and subversive teachings, but the apostasy has not completely taken over yet and the love of Christ and the truth is growing stronger in some.

Looking at the rest of the world we see Israel surrounded by Moslem enemies that overwhelmingly out number them. The main difference in Islam and Christianity is that Islam teaches that Jesus is not the divine Son of God but was only a prophet. A main theme is that Christians and Jews have corrupted Allah's word, and he has sent Mohammed as a prophet to set the record straight. Christians and Jews are to be tolerated if they don't make trouble, but they are not Allah's favored ones. Now Israel has stolen land that is no longer theirs and must be destroyed. Islam requires that those who submit to the faith practice the prescribed pattern of life set forth in the Koran but have the duty to defend the faith at all costs and anything can be forgiven if done in defense of the faith. Anything done to destroy Israel is seen by many as commended by Allah and rewarded in heaven.

Here in America, we have gone from a nation where the church believed in the truth of the Bible and Jesus as our personal savior to a land where many have forsaken Him and are now following Satan's lead. The principles of faith, sexual morality, and family that once defined our culture are now rejected by many. Every means of cultural influence is now largely under the control of secularism. We are losing our power and influence in the world and our wealth is being diverted to build up communist China. Many of our most powerful leaders are under the delusion that when Christianity and Christian culture is destroyed secularism will lead us into a glorious new era of human enlightenment and this delusion is leading us to resemble Sodom and Gomorrah more than God's people.

Europe is on the same path, believing that as the world develops, socialist propaganda will lead to an ideal secular humanist world as communism "mellows" under its persistent influence.

China has become the world's most far reaching and all-encompassing propagandist, and the actions of the leadership serve as a perfect example of how propagandists are always motivated to act diametrically opposite to the intent of their efforts at indoctrination to achieve their goals. The Fabian socialist community in America and Europe has hatched the idea that a new unified secular world would be developed by "globalism", that is, exporting American industry to the underdeveloped world. Theoretically, as they develop, cultural exchange and a feeling of interdependence will enable socialist propagandists to draw the whole world together with their indoctrinating influence. China has taken full advantage of this by developing a form of capitalist economy, under communist government control, to show the world that communism works better than capitalism. Now, we've become dependent on them and pay them for just about everything we use.

America has become more collectivist thinking and poorer while China has become more capitalist and richer. The weakest link they have is the one child policy, which they are trying to change. Domestic prosperity really depends on a growing population and the government is going to have a hard time convincing people to have more children when they have gotten used to the lack of expense and responsibility and a government that has assumed the responsibility for indoctrinating them.

The Soviet Union, which had been the greatest perceived threat to personal freedom in the world for many years, finally collapsed in 1991. After about seventy years of the dictatorship of the proletariat, the Russian leadership, wanting to move the union forward to real accomplishment, realized that the people under communism had no incentive or personal initiative and conceded that it had been a failure.

Lack of personal responsibility became a habitual trait in the lifestyle of people living under communist control and shifting to a new economy was difficult. Eventually Russia came under the domination of a totalitarian oligarchy wanting to restore it back to the territorial sovereignty of the old Soviet Union. Individual freedom and fairness were mighty fleeting in Russia. The constitution allows the practice of one's religious faith, but the government now sees the Christian faith as a potential threat to their control and laws have been passed that make it a crime with severe punishment to evangelize. They can go to church if that's their belief. but cannot make any public effort to draw anyone else to their beliefs.

A passage in Revelation gives an eerie description of a deceived world in the last days. "Woe to the inhabiters of the earth and of the sea! For the devil is come down to you, having great wrath, because he knoweth that he hath but a short time." (Rev. 12:12) Here the devil is cast out of heaven and comes here in seething fury because he knows his fate and is determined to spite Christ by deceiving as many as he can to draw us away from Him.

I will not attempt to be an interpreter of the order, symbology, and time frame of Revelation, but we should all be able to determine that the things described as last events are all clearly seen in the world now. The earth is controlled by political entities with an agenda to remake the world that cannot be completed until the belief in Christ is destroyed.

Notice one thing about the world's animosity toward the Christian faith. When God established Israel as His nation of people, He commanded that they were to be a peculiar people. Something about them was to be distinctive and different. They were to follow His set of rules, to meditate on them, love the Lord and His ways, and it would result in a different culture. The difference would set them apart from the rest of the world. Later, Christians received the same instruction.

When the world, inspired by the devil, attacks Christianity it doesn't attack the creed we received from God. It offers a distraction and attacks Christians as deceived and resistant to the devil's version of good because we are under a delusion that God is real. If the devil can keep people away from anything that God actually said, it's a lot easier to convince them that believing in a God they can't see will lead them to strange and delusional behavior. Then he can lead them to beliefs and behavior that really is strange, delusional, and destructive. If he focused on what would happen if people really followed Christ and tried to contradict it, that would only lead to the conviction that God is right. The devil is trying to lead us away from the path of real security and wisdom and divert our attention to other channels where he can fool us.

He has gone to an amazing amount of intricate scheming and work to prepare those he fools to resist the gospel, and believers to use the things of the world, instead of the gospel, to resist him. Recently I heard a young lady in a news program talking about the controversy over allowing biological males who want to identify as female to compete in girls' sports. She said that her position was not anti-trans but pro woman. The devil has most of us conditioned to respond to his challenges the same way, as if acknowledging that his side is at least right to some extent and any objection should be offered apologetically in that spirit.

The real problem here is that the devil has managed to change us from a culture where God's wisdom is publicly and privately taught and understood to one where it is not. A lot more needs to be said when only the Holy Spirit speaks, and has our attention, as in church and at home, to get a sense of His rules and our duty to implant them firmly in our minds and our culture. We also need a basic unity and purpose to work beyond the walls of the church to build a society that is publicly exposed to the way of thinking that God wants to implant in us. That will require coordination and direction that can only come from the Holy Spirit.

If the devil can keep us away from the voice of God and into the institutions he influences, he can eventually convince us of almost anything. He understands the childish irresponsibility of the sin nature and with enough time away from the Holy Spirit, he can lead us step by step to angry rebellion against good sense and against God.

Much of the younger generation has been lured away from God's truth into the devil's mirage where responsibility is strictly the burden of society. Many now give no thought to any requirement of personal moral constitution. Instead, they identify rightness as the political correctness of the media's spin doctors and hold the attitude they conjure of those not in alignment in disdain. We need to be working now in a concentrated effort to expose them every way we can to understanding the psychology of God's ways.

We are now near the end of the age, and the way America is being led will have serious repercussions. Throughout history cultural decline has brought about turmoil and upheaval. Whether people benefit or suffer depends on whether they blame their sin and turn to God, or whether they place the blame based on the devil's accusations and let him lead them farther. The devil is working furiously to see to it that the things of Christ are shunned, and ultimately will be blamed when a corrupted culture fails. But people can understand the truth if you can get their attention, and the church should be equipped to communicate the wisdom of the Holy Spirit and always use it well regardless of the spirit of the times. We never know at the time what turn of events signify the beginning of the end.

Chapter 22

Empowerment and Understanding

I believe the Lord wants to send a great revival in America before He comes. I believe He wants to see His church, those who still hold to the fundamentals of the faith and trust His word, to come together in purpose and prayer, seeking His will for establishing a more united and effective evangelical force.

Many of the mainstream churches are experiencing schism under pressure and the church in general is coming under harsh criticism as the media moves the general culture away from the traditional Christian way of thinking. A lot of Americans, including many in the church, are getting confused about what it means to be a Christian anymore. The world is getting its' way deeply ingrained in the peoples' minds and as the voice of God is being drowned out the church in America is becoming disjoined, confused, and impotent.

If we would have a real revival, we need to be united with a clear understanding of what we are trying to revive and what has corrupted us away from that. The true Christian life is about spirituality. The Holy Spirit is given to everyone that repents of sin and accepts Jesus as personal savior. He is the spirit of God Himself, sent to dwell within you because you are unable of your own strength and wisdom to overcome the challenges and deceptions of the devil. To receive Him you must have a deep, personal love of Jesus. The church is here to lead you to that and see to it that you keep it.

It is a spiritual message that if you will be truthful with God and ask Him, He will come into your heart and give you the spiritual transformation you need for everlasting life. For Him to do that you must have faith, and to have faith you must be focused on the Holy Spirit and the wisdom and truth of God's word.

Without the guidance of the Holy Spirit the devil will lead you to accept his version of right and wrong which will tell you that you are just fine like you are and you will resent any suggestion that you aren't. He will soon have you conditioned to subconsciously and automatically think that what you need is never the overcoming of personal sin but the destruction of anything that gets in the way of your personal pride, completely oblivious to the spirit of truth. That is the habitual pattern of thought that many in America are developing as they are led away from spiritual understanding.

The main reason many churches are ineffective today is because they have allowed false teachers to gain position and power to direct attention toward secular thinking to better our world instead of the Holy Spirit. No church can draw people to Jesus in the personal way the Bible says to come if they've been taught to believe that the Bible should not be taken literally. Neither can they believe in divine inspiration and authority if they are taught that some of it is meaningful but some not applicable in the present. There is no way you can teach this without tacitly admitting that you don't believe the Bible yourself and are only using it as a pretext for teaching your own ideas. It only draws them into the self-pride and fruitless way of thinking the devil uses to deceive and ensnare the world. They will ignore the Holy Spirit and look to their own ideas. Eventually any guidance from the church will not seem important to them and their support will dwindle to nothing. They will have missed everything the church was meant to give them.

The entire purpose of Jesus coming to us and dying on a cross is to draw us away from this carnal world to the spiritual and the only way we can continue His work is through the power of the Holy Spirit. When you have preachers being trained by those who are teaching them that much of the Bible is not really true, and therefore not inspired by the Holy Spirit who is able to furnish our needs, what can you expect?

We have to make up our minds one way or the other; Do we have a Spiritual God who spoke to us offering truth, wisdom, and guidance or did the Bible result only from the attempts of men to do those things? Do we have something real that we can trust and be enthused about or are we just left to figure it all out for ourselves? The church was founded on the belief that the Bible is true and the foundation we have in Christ is real.

If we're going to get away from that it cannot last.

Jesus warned against calling Him Lord without heeding His voice. In Luke 6:46-49 He describes those who would build a church on any other foundation. The house they are building will fall when the elements come against it. The woke church that listens to the voice of the world instead of Christ will soon disintegrate.

The church in America is now at a critical juncture. I believe our Lord wants the leadership of those who trust in His word to not be lured into the comfort zone the devil is preparing, heed the warning given to the church of Laodicea, and take a firm position. I believe He wants his church organized to make an all-out concerted effort to bring this land back to Him. I believe He will supply us with empowerment and understanding if we will come together acknowledging the authority of the Holy Spirit over us.

I believe He wants fundamentalist leaders to begin an attempt to band the whole church of true believers together in an organized effort to find effective ways to spread the gospel in the present cultural environment; an association of churches seeking the guidance of the Holy Spirit for a mutually shared plan of evangelism. I'm sure there are many ways to break through the firewall the devil's channels of influence seem to have on the younger generation today and get our message across.

This association should have, as an initial agenda, a meeting of the minds about the core elements of the faith; a good outline of the parameters of tolerance we should have for different denominational interpretations of scripture and manners of worship. Almost everything that separates us now is a matter of one thinking the other is too far to the left and the other thinking he is too far to the right. If we really had to settle it in open debate with Jesus serving as referee, we might wind up feeling a bit sheepish by His verdicts. A little open discussion when we have come together to seek the will of the Holy Spirit for the work He has given us might leave us all more enlightened and tolerant of the amount of importance others place on points of doctrine. Those things that are clearly in violation of Christian doctrine must be avoided by making sure the churches that accept them are not included in the association. If we are going to revive the Christian faith it can only be done by Christians, and we must be very clear about what must be central and what variations of interpretation are acceptable to that.

I don't think it will be a problem getting different Christian denominations to work in unity. If we pray and faithfully follow the guidance of the Holy Spirit, I honestly believe that He will show us many things that we could not do as individual churches or denominations to enlarge our outreach. We can still do as much as ever within our own churches but will increase the power of the whole church as the voice of Christ with all denominations still able to maintain their own integrity and characteristics.

This type of organization could open up endless possibilities to evangelize that we are missing entirely in our present fragmented state. What if, for instance, instead of America being exposed almost solely to documentaries on television claiming as science their theories that the Bible is based on fiction, we were often presenting our case in the same manner that it is true? The devil uses every means of communication to subliminally inculcate us to accept the cultural changes that lead us away from Christ. What if we were able to use the same channels to present clear reasoning that his way is destroying us, and Christ's will save us? It is plain to anyone who will be honest with himself, but he needs to hear it, and if he won't go to church he needs to hear it somewhere else. Lack of exposure to reason and logic is the greatest cause of deserting God and the resulting cultural collapse in America today, especially among children and young adults. The devil has free rein to draw us into his way subconsciously because we just simply see it daily as the accepted norm and are blinded to the truth of how the human mind really works and where lack of spiritual wisdom leads us.

With unity and organization our voice could carry a lot more weight in many ways. Church members would be encouraged and emboldened, and others would take notice, because we would acquire an image of more power and influence. We could more effectively protest things that adversely affect our culture, conduct pro-Christ movements, influence the direction of public opinion, and advertise, coordinate, and air revivals better.

I believe the Lord has laid it on my heart to suggest that the church come together in an organized front because that is needed to overcome the obstacles we face today. In Chapter 14, I mentioned two things holding back the Holy Spirit's work, the abundance of material things and the volume of "information" we deal with. These are more pervasive distractions than we tend to realize, and the devil uses them well. We must be ever aware that the devil's strategy to defeat Christ is to change the culture so that people give less thought to real wisdom by distracting them. If we want to lead them back to church we have to make them see spiritual wisdom again. We have to extend our influence beyond the church walls, but it must be done in our charge as the voice for Christ, calling people to think honestly and wisely. We don't need to be sending the "God's gonna get you" kind of message that the non-religious element of American society expects to hear and dismiss with annoyance. They need to hear clear common sense about where we are being led and they need to hear it enough to sink in. Then they can be opened to receive Christ and the Holy Spirit.

In the current state of disunity the church has little power to act in this capacity, but I believe if we come together earnestly asking Him the Holy Spirit will lead us in this, and we will see a great revival and spirit filled churches again.

Chapter 23

Be Strong

A s he closes out his letter to the Ephesian church Paul tells them to be strong and use the power the Lord gives them. Remember again verse 6:12,

"For we wrestle not against flesh and blood, but against principalities, against powers, against the rulers of the darkness of this world, against wickedness in high places."

Then he tells them to put on the whole armor of God. This is something the church needs to take very seriously today. Because some of the church seems to have forgotten it, we've lost a lot of ground to the devil's powers of deception. You're not just in a minor misunderstanding that can be ironed out by both sides listening and trying to understand the other. You're in an all or nothing conflict that will only end when Jesus comes back to this earth. The devil wants you to not believe it, but he is waging a real spiritual war. The church today needs to put on the whole armor of God and be skilled in the use of every weapon we have. We will not win if we are not organized into an effective, well-armed and well-trained army under the leadership of the Holy Spirit.

When attacked, it is not as the ones who believe it better to be baptized than sprinkled or the ones whose worship seems too loud and boisterous with amens or shouts coming from the congregation. The clear goal of the army we face is the total destruction of the church and the worship of Christ on earth. There are many differences in the manner of worship in the various Christian denominations but the final objective of every attack against us all is the same and is part of the same strategy. The goal is always to overwhelm us with the voice of secularism, convolute and weaken our spiritual understanding, and when we are weakened to the point of ineffectiveness in disunity, to destroy us.

We have not been the kind of formidable foe that we should be opposing the devil because we have failed to recognize that we are called on to fight him in unity. Most of us have been simply staying in our own little church and watching the average age of the congregation increase with each passing year.

A little of our budget goes to missionary efforts overseas, but the greatest need for a missionary effort now is right here in America. To make it effective we will have to outthink and outtalk the devil's army. That can only be done if we come together, united in the power of the Holy Spirit. We may have differences, but we all know that there are some fundamentals we must all believe and should be willing to defend and spread to those around us.

There are millions here today who don't believe in a thing in the world that motivates them to any purposeful existence. They are starving for the truth of the gospel, and if it were imparted to them, would be eternally grateful Instead, they are just left alone in the path of the deceiver. The church has failed them, because we didn't realize we needed to be tougher, and we let ourselves be deceived.

The Christian church in America had better wake up and realize what is going on. Most of Europe today is not Christian. Christians are being persecuted in many parts of Asia and Africa, and the devil has put many of us to sleep here. We need to take an honest look at what's happening. The devil has successfully carried out his strategy of subversion and destruction, day by day, to change us from a nation of people with a zeal for Christ to a nation with us in a tiny minority. And there are many now who may have a church affiliation to whom our Lord could only say, "I never knew you."

Seventy years ago, secular newsmen, columnist, etc., were afraid to risk saying anything that might be construed by the public as disparaging to the church. Forty years ago, they didn't hesitate to express opposition and impatience with "fundamentalist" Christianity. Now they are curtly disdainful and hostile to the whole faith. The devil is getting ever more sure of final victory.

A lot of what I've said in this book, identifying those the devil has deceived and made the enemies of the church, may sound like strong, inflammatory speech, but it needs to be said. The voice of God tells us not to practice animosity toward others, but confronting the voice of the devil is necessary. When it goes unchallenged, millions who could have been led to the truth will only be led to ruin. Every sincere Christian needs to be completely aware that there is a plan being followed to destroy the church and the worship of

God in America. But we can't fight it effectively if we only allow ourselves to be stirred to an attitude of vengeful anger. Neither can we afford to be discouraged and do nothing. We have to be the church that we are called to be.

We can win this war if we will, as the body of Christ, come together, united in zeal for our Lord, asking and trusting that He direct us and let the Holy Spirit fill us again. It is my hope and prayer that these thoughts will move those I believe the Holy Spirit is already preparing to be His leaders in the next great revival to begin the work of bringing us together as a great force for Christ that the Holy Spirit will move to victory.

Can you imagine the power of a truly united church with all of our leadership and congregations working and praying together, united in purpose under the power of the Holy Spirit? Can you imagine us carrying out a persistent strategy to bring spiritual revival just as faithfully as the leftist media carries out theirs?

I believe that the Lord really is sympathetic toward us. Mankind from the beginning has faced the constant, deceptive influence of the devil's voice, but the generations in the closer modern world have faced more of his devices coming at us from all directions at once than any before us. We were warned by Jesus that we would face powerful deception in the last days. We have fallen victim to some of Satan's best planned and well-orchestrated schemes and he is fervently pursuing them at this moment.

Still, I believe that if the churches that have grown lukewarm will turn in honest repentance to Christ, ask him, and work for revival, He will lead us. Don't you want to see peace, sanity, and the reverence for Christ restored to this land? It can happen, and I believe that we can have a tremendous, powerful revival if God's people and church leaders will be zealous for His pure word and seek the leadership of the Holy Spirit again.

"Though I walk in the midst of trouble, thou wilt revive me; thou shalt stretch forth thine hand against the wrath of thine enemies, and thy right hand shall save me. The Lord will perfect that which concerneth me." Psalms 135:7-9

Epilogue

R evival is all about bringing the church back to what was furnished for us in the beginning, Christ and the Holy Spirit. They are still the same. If we want a revived nation, we must come wholly back to following them to make the voice of God heard again.

When a nation refuses to hear the voice of God the devil will lead them to believe that real peace and prosperity can come only after his enemy is destroyed. He will try to misdirect and cloud their perception, but that enemy is Christ and the church.

He is now leading America to abandon the church because of the sinister attitude and objectives he conjures and associates with traditional Christian culture. He begins in an oblique manner but from the start his aim is the destruction of the church. This scheme in America is already long past the beginning stage, the attack on "fundamentalism", and now openly directed toward our complete destruction.

The way he leads blinds us to personal responsibility into misguided reliance on the governance of a self-determinist society. When we lose sight of the God who took personal responsibility for us and set that for our example, we are led away from the real love of others and recognition that they have the same rights and desire for self-expression, achievement, and success as we. We are led into resentment, envy, hatred, and the attempted destruction of others' successes. We lose all sight of self-examination and genuine concern for others. We become conditioned by attitude, not reason, and spiteful of all whose attitudes we perceive to conflict with ours. This becomes our national moral character.

This is the way most of the media in America is leading us today. We need to learn the way and attitude of Christ. America cannot change from the puerile and destructive path we are on now until more of us change our way of thinking. It can be done, though, and will make a tremendous difference for the better.

The devil knows the paramount thing he must do now is keep us away from the understanding and wisdom that the Holy Spirit imparts. He will try to block that in every way possible.

The church today faces the most concentrated and organized force in history, bent on our destruction, and we are in no way organized to fight it. The main resistance the devil faces is the kind he is best prepared to handle; people angry at other people he has deceived and used instead of him. He is the master of deception. It is really quite easy for him to keep us, when we are not following Christ, fervently fighting each other with worldly means and unaware of the real war he is waging.

Most of us have been inured to accept the separation of church and state, and when practiced in its original intent, that is a good thing. Our faith should come from a sincere pursuit of truth and the evangelizing of earnest believers, not a government that tells us what we must practice.

But many of us think of "church" as something that should exercise powers of influence within its walls and "state" as everything else in the secular world where we are not supposed to intrude. The devil wants us to believe that every tool he uses in the secular culture is outside the realm of the church and we have no right to use the same things.

The danger we face is not from a government telling us what faith to practice. It is from a force within the secular world that wants to destroy our faith and eventually gain enough control of secular culture that the state will tell us we can no longer practice any faith. They want us intimidated to think we have no right to influence secular culture while they work relentlessly within it to destroy the church.

The purpose of separation of church and state is to allow us to search for what belief is best for personal and social welfare with the right to freely practice, express, and disseminate it. Maintaining a culture that facilitates that is necessary and government should not interfere.

Christians have a duty to practice, express, and spread the gospel. Jesus wants us to bring the message of His salvation to the whole world. The more successful we are at doing that, the more the Holy Spirit will impart wisdom and peace. Can we not see how the nation rages in lunacy as we abandon Christ?

If we want to regain the power and eminence of the church we need to come together and act as a united force. I believe the Lord wants the fundamentalist evangelical faction of the church to form an association to unite us in prayer led purpose and seek His direction for extending our outreach and influence through every means available to us. The devil has not achieved his level of success at corrupting America spasmodically. It was carried out as a well-planned and organized operation. The church needs organization, cooperation, and shared strategy to counter it.

America's spiritual decline has corresponded with a cultural decline. The devil is well aware that he must change the cultural surroundings to destroy the church. What we are seeing in America today is the same thing that drew Israel away from Jehovah and caused Him to scatter them. It is why we are losing a generation now. If we don't fight him on the battlefield where he attacks how can we expect to win? The covenant that Israel had with Jehovah was that they would not only put Him first in their hearts individually but would establish, practice, and jealously guard a culture where He was openly acknowledged, and His precepts were the law of the land. The war today is not just about seeing to it that those who happen to believe in Christ have the right to worship Him if that is their wish. It is about who is going to have controlling influence in the surrounding culture. Both God and Satan understand the power of that completely. We need to bring America back to a Christian culture and the church back to a force that will maintain and nourish it.

The church was started by the faithful believers after the resurrection of Christ. They were united in purpose, sought the coordination of the Holy Spirit, and acted under His power. They were in a national and world culture just as foreboding as we are facing now.

We can be successful at bringing revival to the modern church only through the power and direction of the Holy

Spirit. He is the only power given to us. He is God living in us. He gives wisdom and understanding to see that the devil's way leads to ruin and Christ's to eternal life and blessing. He can bring America to repentance and renew our way of thought and action.

Our enemy will do all in his power to convince us that nobody in the modern world will believe a spiritual message. He wants us to believe that if we want people to listen to anything we say it needs to be a weak and diluted gospel that is really just an altered version of the same path the liberal media is leading us down today. He is determined to keep us, especially the younger generation, from the truth of the Holy Spirit.

We must realize that we are in a full-scale spiritual war and the devil is dead-serious about it. We will certainly be resisted. When he sees that we are actually making inroads he will try to stir up opposition to a frenzy.

If we are unwilling to face that we might as well not start. But if we are dedicated and willing to completely trust Him when challenged the Holy Spirit will lead us into a great revival.

When a person is led to Christ that is the most valuable thing that ever happens to him. There are millions around us today who need Him more than anything else, so let's get started using the power given to us like the earlier church and bring this land back to Him.

Let's revive the church in America!